Dedication

After quite a bit of thought, I decide people who serve their country in th Thousands of them have served year some with their lives. Since 1963 the

CW01500416

in the dark. But only a very small amount of rogues at the top were in on the unconscionable killing of the 35th President of the United States of America. It was the list of characters, all mentioned in this book, that were responsible for the act that has been hidden for over 60 years now. None of those involved in the execution of President Kennedy are still alive. There is no person in any of the agencies who could be connected in any way. So why do they continue to work to hide the facts and the truth? The unofficial motto of the Central Intelligence Agency is on Wikipedia. And ye shall know the truth and the truth shall make you free. (John 8:32)

Motto: The work of a Nation. The Center of Intelligence. And ye shall know the truth and the truth shall make you free. (John 8:32)

Over 20 thousand employees Free. (John 8:32)

CONTENTS

PATRIOTISM

UNHINGED

1963 - 2024

By James Manning

About the Author

James Manning, Born July 13, 1943, Pittsburgh, PA. Graduated Central Catholic High School. Old Dominion University, Successfully completed Virginia Board of Bar Examiners Law Reading Program. Served in the United States Marine Corps, honorably discharged. Was invited to the Olympic Trials for Track and Field, representing the Marine Corps.Honorary Colonel in the Norfolk, VA Sheriff's Dept. Past President of the Ancient Order of Hibernians, Order of the Tower. Knights of Columbus 4th Degree. Small Business Adviser. Married to Bernice. Father to 2 daughters: Shannon Manning and Erin Manning. 1 Granddaughter: Lily Easter.

Page Blank Intentionally

FOREWARD

Why Would The United States Murder Their Own President?

We look to books to resolve the decades-long debate over the gunshots that killed JFK on that historic day in Dallas years ago. All the books that debate the facts, including dissecting the minutia, like angles of the presidential kill shot or the who's who of professional hitmen invited to Dallas that day, while interesting, are distractions from the truth.

Before and after the definitive 888-page Warren Commission Report was released on Oswald as the sole assassin, the CIA was on a covert mission to squash the debaters' stories, interviews, and books. It was J. Edgar Hoover, head of the FBI, who advised the CIA opératives to let all the debaters take the floor. The more debates, books, and research from ordinary citizens, the better for the executioners — bury the truth and let confusion reign.

The cover-up of the JFK assassination started months before the day Kennedy was killed. The patsy who would take the fall for the crime was specifically chosen by James Angleton, Chief of Counterintelligence at the 1963 CIA. Why Oswald? It was a last-minute decision of circumstance, and the sloppiness of that decision shows.

I decided to write this book to tell my story about an Oswald fact that will change history.

This book includes reprints of meticulously coordinated meeting minutes distributed among a small group of government officials between March 1963 and December 1963 and led by James Angleton and Robert Crowley, the Deputy Director of Clandestine Operations for the CIA, to plan the assassination of John F. Kennedy. Shocking.

Robert Crowley co-authored *The New KGB: Engine of Soviet Power,* released in 1985. CIA operations during the Kennedy administration resemble those of President Putin of Russia, a KGB-trained foreign intelligence officer.

Maybe, like me, you ask yourself, who would want the President of the United States eliminated? And who would fund such an articulate planned operation? What was the 1963 budget to kill an American President? Line item for mercury-filled bullets = $500. Line item for hitmen = $400,000? Texan oil barons funded the assassination alongside American taxpayer money, which funds the CIA and other agencies.

On December 22, 1963, one month after Kennedy's murder, it was former President Harry Truman who knew the truth. In a column written for The Washington Post, the headline speaks volumes to the men who killed Kennedy: *Limit CIA Role to Intelligence.*

Truman, who created the Central Intelligence Agency, makes clear in the article, "For some time, I have been disturbed by the way the CIA has been diverted from its original assignment. It has become an operational and, at times, a policy-making arm of the Government."

Based on this author's extensive research, the agency began using cloak-and-dagger operations to make judge-and-jury decisions and redefined treason in the process. So why would the Kennedy family not invest in knowing the truth? Because the last thing they wanted was for Kennedy's legacy to be treason.

As we come to grips with uncomfortable truths about America's foreign policy and intelligence agencies during the Cold War, and especially today when we can do something about it, any new light shed on covert activities and the facts of Lee Harvey Oswald is welcomed by all who want a healthy American democracy in the future.

I wrote this book for curious people who know nothing about the Kennedy assassination, for the people who know everything about it, and for everybody in between.

Chapter 1

Lee Harvey Oswald received the Marines Designation

"UNQ"

And Failed to Qualify as Rifleman

Oswald was Not the JFK Shooter

I enlisted in the Marine Corps in 1961. I was serving in the 1st Marine Battalion, 2nd Marine Division, on November 22, 1963, when President Kennedy was assassinated. I was in shock and heartsick like the rest of the world, and glued to any TV or radio for more information. I accepted the Warren Report when it came out and, like most people, moved on. In 1964, my tour in a rifle company was over, and I accepted a transfer to Headquarters Marine Corps in Arlington, Virginia.

I worked in the Navy Annex on Columbia Pike as a clerk in the records section and was billeted at Henderson Hall adjacent to Arlington Cemetary. During the day, I worked with civilians, but when we drew night duty, we were alone from 5 p.m. until 7 a.m. We were there for security, but we doubled as File Clerks and answered the phone if the staff duty officer needed emergency data from the record books if a Marine was injured anywhere in the world.

We had a cot and a TV, but in 1964, there were only three channels, and it could get pretty dull at times. One of the things we used to do to break the monotony was to go down to the Special

Officers Section. It was a small file room inside the football field-size documents building. There, they kept the jackets of the illustrious Marines heroes: Chesty Puller, Dan Daly, Congressional Medal winners, et al.

Now, most of these files were one to two inches thick. I would finger through the files, pick one out, and read the exploits of that particular hero. One night, as I was looking through the file cabinet, I saw what appeared to be an empty folder. I pulled it out, intending to discard it, but I was amazed to see it was labeled Oswald, Lee Harvey. I opened it, and inside were only four or five pages, yet a copy of his DD214 was on top. Every person serving in the Armed Forces is issued this document when separated from active duty. This document provides various veterans benefits.

As I studied the information, my attention was drawn to Section 26. This is where decorations, medals, commendations, badges, and awards are listed, as well as Rifle Qualification. The Marine Corps has three levels of qualification: Expert, Sharpshooter, and Marksman. **Oswald received the designation "UNQ," the acronym for Marines who failed to qualify as Rifleman.** Had he ever qualified while on active duty, the highest level would be the one shown. I was fully aware of what I was looking at; **Lee Harvey Oswald could have never made three shots in Dallas, let alone one.**

It was common knowledge that if you didn't qualify as a Rifleman, you would go to a motor pool, become a cook, or be assigned to an air wing, like the one in Astugi, Japan, where Oswald was once assigned.

The next event occurred when Jim Garrison announced that he was going to indict Clay Shaw as part of the conspiracy to assassinate President Kennedy. Besides my family and a few close friends, I never shared what I had seen in that file. I decided this was the time to reveal what I believed was a small yet important detail in that case.

In April 1968, I reached Jim Garrison's office in New Orleans, and after going through several assistants, I told them I had some information that might be important to this case. Garrison picked up the phone. First, I was impressed with his refined manner and easy way of asking me questions. I offered that I was part of a study group on the assassination at Old Dominion, and we would love to have him speak there sometime. He said he would love to come when the trial was over.

I started to say that I had seen something that I wasn't supposed to see, but he abruptly stopped me from saying anything else. He said something to the effect that the phone line might not be secure. He instructed me to call back in two weeks, and we broke off the call.

A few days later, an article appeared in the local paper, The Virginian Pilot, with a picture of Garrison and a story about his conversation with me and agreeing to speak at Old Dominion. I was shocked to see it and can only assume someone from his office called the paper.

At the time, I had a job at a jewelry store in Norfolk, Virginia. The part-time watchman there was very strange. He never spoke to anyone but the manager. I asked the manager why he had a .357 Magnum under a towel on his bench. The manager said he was some government *spook* and worked for the army down south. Yet he is excellent at fixing watches and locks.

Several days after the article appeared in the paper, I arrived at work, and the Spook called me over with two fingers. I looked around to see if he was motioning to someone else; he wasn't. It was me he wanted. I walked over to him. He slid off his stool, got nose to nose with me, and said, "If you know what's good for you, you'll leave the fucking Kennedy thing alone. Do you understand me?" I'll be honest — he made a hell of an impression on me. I said nothing and tried not to let him know I was concerned.

Yet, I decided to try to find out something about him. He was born in Norfolk, Virginia, and his family owned the Sansone vegetable stand for years, only a few blocks from the jewelry store. His name was Antonio (or Vincent) Sansone.

I later learned that Sansone worked for the NARF, the Naval Air Rework Facility, and became friends with Frank Fiorini, who also worked there. They enjoyed flying and worked together in bars in Norfolk. For 18 months, Fiorini managed the Havana-Madrid tavern that catered to foreigners, primarily Cuban merchant seamen.

I learned later that Frank Fiorini changed his name to Sturgis when his mother remarried. It is well documented today that Sturgis was a longtime CIA operative and eventually became Fidel Castro's right-hand man during the successful Cuban revolution. Sturgis also trained fighters and led the Bay of Pigs invasion against the Castro regime. Many researchers believe Sturgis was in Dallas on the day of the assassination. Although there are varying accounts that insist Sturgis bragged about killing JFK, he also denied he had anything to do with the Dallas plot. However, Sturgis promoted widespread misinformation, claiming Fidel Castro was the mastermind behind the JFK assassination. Later, Sturgis did time for participating in the break-in at the Watergate, which led to the scandal that eventually ended the presidency of Richard Nixon.

Considering that Sansone was close friends with Sturgis since they met in Norfolk, where I have lived most of my life, it added up to why Sansone kept his gun on him at all times in the jewelry store where I worked. After the jewelry store manager told me Sansone did some work for the Army down south, it would follow that perhaps

Sansone worked with Sturgis as a contract agent for the CIA, and the watchmaker job was a cover.

Reprinted in COUP D'ETAT IN AMERICA VOLUME SIX, by AJ Weberman: *A FBI document dated February 5, 1964, concerning Orlando Bosch read: Synopsis: FRANK Fiorini, admitted associate of William Johnson, denied implication in or any specific knowledge of attempted MIRR air raid December 28, 1963. Dr. Orlando Bosch gave statement to press claiming that bombs would have been dropped on crowds in Havana celebrating 5th anniversary of the revolution on January 2, 1964, had not been seized carrying bombs to secret base in the Caribbean. MM T-1 has advised that Bosch gave this distorted statement to the press for propaganda purposes as MIRR intended only to bomb (deleted) Cuba. MM-T1 also advised that Bosch is presently attempting to raise more money to carry out further bombing raid against Cuba." The FBI interviewed Frank: Fiorini is a personal friend of WILLIAM JOHNSON. About two weeks ago Fiorini was with JOHNSON at Broward International Airport. JOHNSON introduced Fiorini to Charles Bush, who operates an airline charter business at that airport. This was the first and last contact Fiorini had with Bush. After this introduction, JOHNSON went with Bush to the latter's office at the airport, and **Fiorini went to a nearby restaurant where he chanced upon Antonio Sansone, a Cuban exile pilot.** Fiorini said that he did not know the nature of JOHNSON'S business with Bush. He denied specific knowledge of JOHNSON being involved in an air raid attempt in cooperation with ORLANDO BOSCH. He states however, that he knew JOHNSON was "up to something" but he did not know what.*

As I put all this together and realized Sturgis and Sansone lived so close to my proximity, it's hard to put into words how I felt when I realized my life was threatened that day. I had never publicly spoken about what I knew about Oswald until I wrote this book.

5

I called Jim Garrison's office in January 1968 to share my crucial evidence that Oswald was innocent and not the JFK shooter. The Spook at the jewelry store had no idea of the true nature of my call to Garrison. Yet, based on my invitation to Garrison to speak at Old Dominion University located in the heart of Norfolk, where Sansone and his close friend Frank Sturgis lived and owned businesses, I never called Jim Garrison back when the trial was over. Many people who knew anything about the JFK assassination were killed to conceal the truth. Through my ancestry research, I learned that Sansone came from a long line of watchmakers. He moved to Schenectady, New York, until his death in 1987.

For all the people curious about the assassination and the conspiracy to conceal the facts, I believe this small yet significant detail will illuminate the Truth on many levels. The Warren Report implicating Oswald is a work of fiction.

I am 81 years old this year, 2024. As a Marine, Semper Fidelis, always faithful, it is my honor to exonerate Lee Harvey Oswald of the JFK murder.

Jim Manning's Marine Record

MANNING, James Robert Jr.

U. S. Marine Corps   Pittsburgh, Allegheny, Pennsylvania

High School - 4 Yrs

Discharged

Henderson Hall, Arlington, Virginia 22214

Home   Private E-1

1324 Morningside Avenue
Pittsburgh, Allegheny, Pennsylvania

0141 - Administrative Man   Typist (clerical)

Good Conduct Medal (1st Award)
Sharpshooter Rifle Badge

Camp Lej., N. C.   7 Wks - 1943   Admin Sool   MOS: Marine MOS

No time lost current active duty
Enure leave from: 3Oct64 To: 16Oct64; From: 6Dec64 To: 11Dec64; From: 4Apr65 To: 8Apr65
Good Conduct Medal period commenced on 31Oct64
Social Security Number 193-32-7392

1921 C Street, N. W.
Washington, D. C.

James R. Manning

DD FORM 214

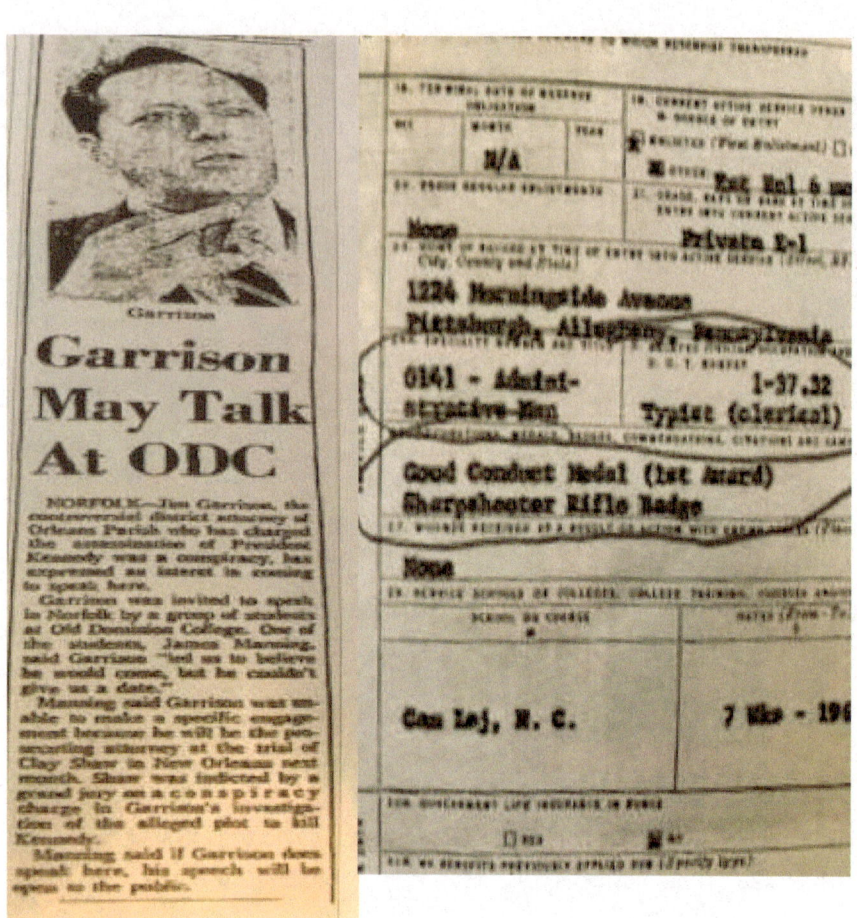

Poster Produced by H.L. Hunt, Oil Baron

WANTED
FOR
TREASON

THIS MAN is wanted for treasonous activities against the United States:

1. Betraying the Constitution (which he swore to uphold):
   He is turning the sovereignty of the U. S. over to the communist controlled United Nations.
   He is betraying our friends (Cuba, Katanga, Portugal) and befriending our enemies (Russia, Yugoslavia, Poland).

2. He has been WRONG on innumerable issues affecting the security of the U. S. (United Nations - Berlin wall - Missle removal - Cuba - Wheat deals - Test Ban Treaty, etc.)

3. He has been lax in enforcing Communist Registration laws.

4. He has given support and encouragement to the Communist inspired racial riots.

5. He has illegally invaded a sovereign State with federal troops.

6. He has consistantly appointed Anti-Christians to Federal office: Upholds the Supreme Court in its Anti-Christian rulings.
   Aliens and known Communists abound in Federal offices.

7. He has been caught in fantastic LIES to the American people (including personal ones like his previous marriage and divorce).

treason | ˈtrēzən | noun
(also high treason) the crime of betraying one's country,

9

Chapter 2

Wanted For Treason

An Excerpt from *Dallas 1963* by Steven Davis and Bill Minutaglio*:*

John and Jackie Kennedy return to their suite at the Hotel Texas at 10 a.m. In forty-five minutes, they will leave for Dallas.

Kennedy's aide, Kenny O'Donnell, comes into the suite with a copy of the Dallas Morning News. The president skimmed the headlines earlier but didn't look through the whole paper. O'Donnell shows him the full-page advertisement denouncing him on page 14. Kennedy reads every word, grimacing. Finished, he hands the paper over to Jackie for her inspection.

He shakes his head and says to O'Donnell: "Can you imagine a paper doing a thing like that?"

A flyer that circulated around Dallas prior to President Kennedy's arrival, claiming he was wanted for treason for "Betraying the Constitution" and for giving "support and encouragement to the Communist-inspired racial riots," among other supposed violations.

Then he turns to Jackie: "Oh, you know, we're heading into nut country today."

Kennedy begins pacing around the hotel room. He stops in front of his wife: "You know, last night would have been a hell of a night to assassinate a President." She gives him a look. "I mean it," he continues. "There was the rain and the night, and we were all getting jostled. Suppose a man had a pistol in a briefcase." He points at a wall with his finger and pretends to shoot: *"Then he could have dropped the gun and the briefcase and melted away in the crowd."*

A few weeks earlier, he'd met in the White House with Jim Bishop, the author of "The Day Lincoln Was Shot." Kennedy said his feelings about assassination were similar to Lincoln's: "Any man who is willing to exchange his life for mine can do so." And now, the ad in Dealey's paper has brought back to the surface a reality he tries to suppress: there are people in America who would like to see him dead. He walks over to a window and looks outside.

"It would not be a very difficult job to shoot the president of the United States," he muses aloud. "All you'd have to do is get up in a high building with a high-powered rifle with a telescopic sight, and there's nothing anybody could do."

H.L. Hunt, a Texan oil tycoon and wealthiest man in the world at the time, paid to have these flyers advertised in the local newspapers and distributed all over Dallas days before Kennedy arrived there for a political event and was assassinated. The politics of extremism flourished in 1960s Dallas. Well-known right-winged men teamed up with lesser-known men and women to bring the scare tactics of the Right Wing to full bloom in Dallas.

Kennedy was shot dead in Dealey Plaza. Newspaper editor Ted Dealey, whose "Dallas Morning News" was often filled with abusive rhetoric towards Kennedy, Adlai Stevenson, Eisenhower, Eleanor Roosevelt, and others in public life whom Dealey didn't "trust" to stay true to the United States Constitution and protect America from the Communist masses.

The John Birch Society, led by H.L. Hunt and Young Americans for Freedom, were only two of the many groups active on the fertile ground of Dallas' political paranoia. Also, there were elements of the Left in Dallas, yet the perceived "Left" wasn't the only faction under fire. There was an assassination attempt against retired general Edwin Walker, who was active in anti-black, anti-Semitic, and anti-Communist groups in the Spring of 1963. Plenty of hate reigned in Dallas to welcome John Kennedy to Dallas when he visited in November 1963. However, the warm welcome the Kennedys received on their arrival and in the streets, the motorcade traveled belied the small-but-vocal hate expressed in the press and political rallies.

Doesn't this political paranoia speak to the same Trump tactics he uses to motivate people that the world is a scary place and inspires the hate he spreads. It works. Yet to what good?

In 1963, the right-wing American business community, like the oil barons, did not achieve extraordinary wealth because they were too busy playing golf. While intelligent, organized, and utterly ruthless, not one of these men would ever risk personally attempting to assassinate a sitting President, knowing full well that if caught, the retaliation would be swift and deadly, not just to their life, but to their legacy; the ultimate humiliation. These men do not get their hands dirty. They pay others to do the dirty work.

So that leaves the gangsters or the government agencies to take out John F. Kennedy.

Chapter 3

The Seed of the Plotters Assassination Plan

To cooperate politely with the Soviet Union and avoid war, President Kennedy regularly maintained close, private communication with Chairman Khrushchev to prevent negative influence from the State Department and the CIA. The President said several times that he did not trust the CIA, which was hell-bent on stirring up a war between the two nations. Many matters that might have escalated due to the Agency's interference were instead settled peacefully through Kennedy's personal contact with Khrushchev to avoid nuclear war.

However, JFK's highly unorthodox personal diplomacy with the Soviets created far more problems for Kennedy than it ever solved. When it came to light via Angleton wiretapping RFK's phone, the DOS and the CIA were extremely concerned that sensitive intelligence matters might have been passed to the Soviets. The fact that RFK, with permission from JFK, was passing what the CIA considered highly secret material to their chief enemy had terrible consequences.

James Jesus Angleton, Chief of the Counterintelligence Department of the CIA, who knew the President and his family socially, was devastated. In private meetings with Angleton's trusted associates, including Robert Crowley, Assistant Director for Clandestine Operations, Angleton made a strong case against Kennedy.

Angleton said the failure of the Bay of Pigs mission was solely the result of Kennedy's moral cowardice. Angleton was initially optimistic that Kennedy fully approved all of the CIA's actions in the Bay of Pigs mission but then blamed others for preserving his reputation. JFK deliberately attacked the CIA's leadership, firing Allen Dulles and his ringleaders and accusing the Agency of bad faith and duplicity.

JFK's negotiations with the head of the Soviet Union behind the back of responsible American government agencies smacked of treason. He undermined all of the intense work the CIA was doing to thwart Soviet imperialism both in Europe and Latin America.

The gravest charge against the President was his behavior in not striking militarily at the armed Soviet troops and their deadly missiles stationed only miles away from American soil. Not only did Kennedy allow the Soviets to get away with their aggression, but he also removed American missiles from Turkey and materially weakened the American military position in Europe. As far as the passing of top secret material to the Soviets was concerned, a furious Angleton claimed that this was high treason and the President must be removed from his high office.

To Kill or Not To Kill — That is The Question

Kennedy was far too popular to institute impeachment proceedings against him in Congress. Leaking information to the CIA's many friendly press sources about the President giving CIA reports to Khruschev was also ruled out. If made public, this information would not only damage Kennedy but also damage the reputation of the CIA and unduly alarm its many highly placed international sources.

Finally, after a series of heated meetings over weeks in February 1963, physical removal was not only broached but also developed. After all, the CIA had been responsible for high-level successful political assassinations in the past in other countries, and they had the means and connections to assist their planning.

Initial plans to blow up the presidential plane were scrapped. Secret Service and U.S. Air Force security were far too comprehensive to permit the clandestine placing of an explosive device on Air Force One.

A second plan was to approach one of the President's physicians, Dr. Max Jacobson, to convince the doctor, who supplied and injected the President with amphetamines, to put certain fatal additives in Kennedy's drugs. The CIA had a small but effective laboratory that specialized in rare poisons. This plan was rejected because it was felt Jacobson was unstable and associated with too many questionable individuals. Using his services would have necessitated removing the doctor as well, and Angleton was firmly against involving more untrustworthy people than necessary in his plot.

Since the President sailed in Massachusetts coastal waters, an assassin could either shoot him at a distance or attach an explosive charge to the hull of his boat. Everyone generally rejected this but Angleton because the President's wife and children might be on board and found unacceptable.

The decision was to shoot the President in the open rather than in a building that could easily be sealed off and immediately searched. Yet if the President was shot in public, the assassin stood a high risk of being captured. If this happened, there was an even worse risk that the attempt could be traced to the CIA.

The CIA , therefore realized that it had to get the support of the entire governmental apparatus to be able to implement such a radical solution to what it considered to be the most severe threat to United States security in decades.

They worked together to ensure the removal of a President who acted against their interests to replace him with a weaker man, Lyndon B. Johnson, whom they believed they could better control. The destruction of the Communist movement in that area was paramount to the CIA and Joint Chiefs, and President Johnson permitted the escalation in Southeast Asia and the Vietnam War. The CIA and Joint Chiefs were hell-bent on war.

Chapter 4

The Corsicans

According to a document found in Robert Crowley's papers, the officially organized assassination of John F. Kennedy by the CIA had the code name: "Operation ZIPPER."

In early March 1963, the actual assassin became a pressing issue among the plotters. Because Crowley's father was a Chicago politician and Parks Commissioner vital in Mayor Kelly-Nash's machine, Crowley had connections with the mob in Chicago, so he was tasked with personally contacting Chicago Mafia members for advice and possible assistance.

Chicago mob leader Sam Giancana, who had assisted in locating persons to carry out the CIA's murder plots against Fidel Castro, loathed the Kennedy brothers but was far too shrewd to lend any of his identifiable men to cooperate in such a project. In two conferences at the Drake Hotel with Crowley, Giancana agreed to locate assassins who perform in a professional manner, suggesting recruitment might be better outside the United States.

Rather than involve the more emotional Sicilian Mafia, Giancana had one of his connections in Italy contact someone in the Corsican Mafia, the Unione Corse in Marseille, to start the recruitment. The assassins were found from the ranks of this more rational criminal organization.

Assassin shopping in Beirut, Lebanon, a center of assassination professionals in 1963, was considered. Yet, the Corsicans would blend in the background in race-conscious Dallas versus the darker-complexioned Lebanese or Arab professionals.

Under no circumstances were the assassins to know of any CIA involvement. They were Giancana's hire. The plotters reasoned that if the killers were captured before the CIA could kill them first, the Corsicans could only identify the Chicago Mafia as their employers. The Mafia would never turn in the CIA as the hiring agent, knowing the CIA would silence them immediately.

The Hitmen

In April 1963, Chicago Mafia boss Sam Giancana advised Crowley that the neutralization job to kill the rogue President required four Corsican hitmen at $100,000 each.

The Scrub

Angleton developed a close working relationship with Israeli intelligence agencies Shabak and Mossad that helped facilitate the plot against Kennedy. As far as Angleton was concerned, the Israeli's sole reason for existence was to ensure that the Corsican assassins were eliminated as soon as possible after their work was done. Angleton contacted Amos Manor, then head of Israeli Counterintelligence and an old friend of Angleton, to scrub the neutralization.

Angleton made it clear, in no way, shape, or form were the Corsicans to know the CIA was involved. They were working solely for the Chicago Mafia, hired by Sam Giancana.

Benjamin Bauman, a terrorist who became a Menachem Begin freedom fighter, was sent to oversee the scrub job. Israel passionately despised JFK because of his firm determination to prevent that state from developing an atomic bomb.

Bauman organized a safe house in Maryland, where after the Corsicans completed the JFK termination, the Corsicans were to be killed and their bodies chopped up and put into crab pots. The bones that the soft-shelled crabs could not eat were to be dumped back into the water. Bones do not float. If true, those human bones can be dug up, and today, their identities are identified with DNA.

Will someone call James Cameron?

The Delivery

Kennedy's visit to Dallas in November 1963 was announced in September. The Angleton assassination plan now ensued with a specific time and geographical location.

In late October, the French-speaking Corsicans were flown to Quebec, Canada, met by Giancana's mafia operatives, and driven over the border to a safe house in Detroit via The Gordie Howe International Bridge. From Detroit, they were flown in a private aircraft to Dallas-Fort Worth.

The Guns

Weapons for the assassination were procured from Sam Cummings, CIA agent and head of INTERARMCO, a proprietary branch of the Agency that specialized in gun-running. Cummings procured two silenced .38-caliber pistols, two 7.65-mm surplus

Argentine army Mausers, and a specially constructed .223-caliber rifle cut down and modified from a standard NATO weapon. Special bullets for the latter weapon, filled with mercury and designed to explode on impact, ensuring immediate death, were manufactured and accompanied the gun. This method is in extensive use by European assassin teams.

The Scapegoat

A check of CIA records located the names of several persons of interest to the Agency in the Dallas area. One was Lee Harvey Oswald, the returned defector, and the other was a well-known CIA operative, the Baltic aristocrat George de Mohrenschildt, who served in a Polish cavalry unit, the Promorski Brigade. Oswald encountered DeMohrenschildt through his connection with the Russian community in Dallas, and he became his mentor and, according to a later CIA classified report, his lover.

Oswald was intimately connected with de Mohrenschildt, which guaranteed that the CIA knew his movements at his residence and in the Dallas area. De Mohrenschildt informed the CIA that Oswald was recently hired at the Texas School Book Depository on October 16, 1963. Angleton realized that this building immediately overlooked the motorcade route Kennedy would take on his November 22 visit to Dallas.

Oswald, the pseudo-defector, had strong connections with the Soviet Union. He married a Soviet citizen and was noticed in public advocating support for Fidel Castro. His position in a tall building overlooking the parade route was a stroke of incredible luck for the plotters. Oswald was the perfect patsy to take the fall for the JFK murder.

Oswald was an afterthought. The CIA was fully prepared with planted witnesses for a murder trial.

All Systems Go

The assassination team was flown to Dallas in early November and spent two weeks accomplishing reconnaissance of the entire presidential route.

The Corsican team leader initially advised that the right-angle turn from Houston to Elm Street would present an excellent target opportunity as the presidential car slowed to make the turn.

The Dallas County Records Building on Houston Street had an excellent line of sight to the Elm Street corner, yet the flanking buildings gave observers a clear view of the shooters. It was finally decided to use the Book Depository as one base.

The railroad overpass was considered another excellent position but was eventually ruled out because it was guarded. To its right, however, the heavy bushes and fences of the elevated "grassy knoll" proved compelling. The official car with the President would be moving slowly past the spot, permitting a slightly downhill shot at very close range. And railroad yards behind the grassy knoll provided an unobserved escape.

The approved assassination team plan was set:

1.   A shooter in the Texas Book Depository, sixth floor.

2.   A shooter in the ornamental bushes just before the underpass.

21

3. Two English-speaking personnel in suits carrying fake law enforcement identification in the railroad yard behind the second shooter to stop anyone who tried to investigate or interfere with the escape of the shooter.

De Mohrenschildt reported that Oswald bought a Mannlicher-Carcano rifle from Klein's Sporting Goods. Both Oswald and his wife mentioned this rifle to de Mohrenschildt, saying it was mailed to Oswald's wife's friend, Ruth Paine, to store in her garage. Oswald never tested the surplus Mannlicher-Carcano Italian army weapon. It was a novelty. He was a lousy shot, and the rifle was never used. Stories about Oswald going to Dallas rifle range with others and firing the Carcano were total fabrications in The Warren Report.

The CIA also put out patently false information about an Oswald visit to Mexico and Cuba, indicating a poorly thought-out attempt to somehow link the assassination to the Soviet Union and Cuba via a dead Oswald. Since the very nervous LBJ frantically expected to avoid any escalation with Russia or Cuba, the phony Mexico City trip was buried in the cobbled-together Warren Commission Report, another reason why the report was dismissed by historians. The Warren Commission Report named Lee Harvey Oswald as the sole assassin.

Before the assassination in mid-1963, on two occasions, French intelligence informed the American Embassy about the recruitment of French underworld operatives in Marseilles for a political assassination in the United States. Whether these reports were passed to Washington or ignored is unconfirmed.

Crow Memo to Angleton: "The Warren Report is a wonderful piece of creative writing"...

To:	JJA
From:	RTC
Date:	August 10, 1964
Subject:	The President

Dear Jim:

The DCI has spoken with me recently concerning several contacts he has had with Jenkins, the President's man.

According to the DCI, the President has been privately expressing his growing concerns that "another Dallas" might be executed against him or his family.

The President is a man who is very easily and badly frightened. He is a highly emotional and very unstable individual who could become quite dangerous if his fears are not addressed.

I spoke with Hoover about this and as a good, personal friend of the President, has agreed to mollify him and put his irrational fears to rest. Hoover has advised the President that certain "negative forces" are at work against those agencies who wish to protect and support the President.

The President has urged Hoover to find a way to "convince " these "troublemakers" to cease their negative remarks "in the best interests" of the nation."

This gives us the opportunity to silence anyone who might express dangerous opinions about Dallas.

Hoover also suggested, and I agree, that instead of attempting to shit down controversial books, we encourage the publication of "not" books. That way, the public will soon grow tired of questions and go on their merry way.

The forthcoming Commission report is a wonderful piece of creative writing and will be extensively promoted by our good friends at the NY Times.

The question of the surviving member is still of concern, but hopefully, the reward will flush him out. I will get Allan to autograph a copy of the final Commission report for both of our personal libraries.

Crow

Allan is Allen Dulles

The Tally

Kennedy was killed on Friday, November 22, 1963.

Oswald was killed on Sunday, November 24, 1963.

Chicago Mafia leader Sam Giancana was shot to death in the basement of his home in June 1975 while cooking sausage and peppers days prior to his testimony before a Congressional committee.

George de Mohrenschildt is alleged to have shot himself just before his scheduled appearance before a Congressional committee in March of 1977.

Rumors are the lead Corsican who blew out the presidential brains at near point-blank range left the scene alone and boarded a commercial bus to Mexico. He ended up in Barcelona, Spain. The name on his passport was Guidobaldo Fini, yet perhaps a fake provided by the CIA.

The other three Corsicans were escorted by Bauman to a two-engined aircraft at a Dallas airfield at 2:30 p.m. on November 22, piloted by a CIA contract pilot, David Ferrie, from New Orleans. It was explained that they would be flown to a safe house in Maryland with a pitstop in New Orleans, where Ferrie was based. They vanished, and Ferrie was the last to see them.

Lucian Sarti

Lucien Sarti worked for the French-Corsican heroin trafficker and convicted Nazi collaborator Auguste Joseph Ricord. Journalist Stephen Rivele, contact Christian David, claims Antoine Guerini organized the assassination of President John F. Kennedy and the kill induced by Sarti and two other members of the Marseilles mob. Some claim Sarti fired from behind the wooden fence on the grassy knoll. The first shot was fired from behind and hit Kennedy in the back. The second shot was fired from behind and hit John Connally. The third shot was fired from in front and hit Kennedy in the head. The fourth shot was from behind and missed. As well as Sarti, David also named Sauveur Pironti and Roger Bocognani as being involved in the killing. However, Pironti and Bocognani both had alibis, and Rivele was forced to withdraw the allegation. Today, Rivele suggests if he were working the case today, he would take a look at Paul Damien Mondoloni, alias Monsieur Paul, a Corsican mafioso who was an important figure of the French Connection. Killed in 1985, Paul Mondoloni was the associate of Marcel Francisci.

When Lucien Sarti was shot dead by police in Mexico City on April 27, 1972, his death went unreported in the United States. However, it was in France's leading newspaper, *Le Monde,* that the killing of Sarti was the result of a "close Mafia-police-Narcotics Bureau collaboration" in the United States to "shatter Corsican influence in worldwide narcotics traffic, to create a virtual monopoly for the U.S.-Italian Mafia connection, whose key figure was Santo Trafficante."

Jean Souetre — Michael Mertz

The journalist Steve Rivele discovered in 1988 that Jean Souètre had an old enemy: Michel Mertz, born in April 1920 (died January 1995), a former member of the French secret services who worked in drug trafficking. Mertz allegedly usurped the identity of Jean Souètre and had the habit of using his name as a pseudonym to possibly compromise Souètre. Or vice versa.

Michel Mertz used two aliases: Jean Souetre and Michel Roux. A man using the name Michel Roux entered the United States on November 19, 1963, and was in Fort Worth on November 22 before leaving the country on December 9.

As a result of investigations carried out by Mary Ferrell and Gary Shaw, which were dismissed, Souetre (or a man using his name) was under arrest in Dallas on the day of John F. Kennedy's assassination. Souetre was immediately released and expelled from the United States.

26

Still unproven, the remaining three CIA-contracted assassins by Giancana were subsequently removed in a crab pot action, and the one who escaped has been the object of intense searches in France and Italy by elements of the CIA.

The Assassins Getaway Pilot — David Ferrie

On November 25, 1963, three days after the assassination, David Ferrie and two other men were booked for vagrancy by the New Orleans district attorney's office, held for investigation by the FBI and Secret Service, and released the next day. Did Ferrie make it to Maryland with the Corsicans? Or was the FBI vagrants investigation another cover?

Garrison Full Circle

William Guy Bannister worked for the FBI and was an assistant superintendent of the New Orleans Police Dept. He was an avid anti-communist, an alleged member of the Minutemen and the John Birch Society, led by H.L. Hunt. On the day of the assassination, Bannister and his employee Jack Martin were drinking together at a local bar. On their return to Banister's office, they got into a heated argument, to which Martin incited him, saying, "What are you going to do – kill me like you all did Kennedy?" Banister drew his revolver and pistol-whipped Martin, sending him to the hospital. In the ensuing days, **Martin told police that (via Bannister) Ferrie was supposed to be the getaway pilot in the assassination.**

Catching wind of the shenanigans, Jim Garrison, New Orleans District Attorney, alleged David Ferrie was involved in the JFK assassination. Garrison also alleged that Ferrie knew Lee Harvey

Oswald. Ferrie denied any involvement in a conspiracy and said he never knew Oswald.

Garrison's aide, Lou Ivon, stated that Ferrie telephoned him the day after the story of Garrison's investigation broke and told him: "You know what this news story does to me, don't you? I'm a dead man. From here on, believe me, I'm a dead man."

On February 22, 1967, less than a week after the newspaper *New Orleans States-Item* broke the story of Garrison's investigation into Ferrie, Ferrie was found dead in his apartment. Garrison said he considered Ferrie's death a suicide but added, "I am not ruling out murder."

Ferrie's autopsy was performed by Orleans Parish coroner Nicholas Chetta and pathologist Ronald A. Welsh. They concluded that there was no evidence of suicide or murder and that Ferrie died of a massive cerebral hemorrhage due to a congenital intracranial berry aneurysm that had ruptured at the base of his brain.

On March 1, 1967, Garrison had Shaw arrested and charged him with conspiring to assassinate Kennedy.

Chapter 5

Final Zipper Meeting — Successful Removal of JFK

for Treason

Reprinted from The Crowley Documents in Regicide

Summary Minutes of the CIA Conference

Date: 22 Dec 63

Reference: Operation ZIPPER

Participants: DCI McCone, James Angleton, Robert Crowley, William Harvey, DD/FBI Sullivan, LtCol Cass, USMC

Distribution as above

Short Bios of the JFK Assassination Planners Operation

Zipper:

1. John Alexander McCone was an American businessman and politician who served as Director of Central Intelligence from 1961 to 1965, during the height of the Cold War.

2. James Jesus Angleton was an American intelligence operative who served as chief of counterintelligence for the Central Intelligence Agency from 1954 to 1975. According to Director of Central Intelligence Richard Helms, Angleton was "recognized as the dominant counterintelligence figure in the non-communist world."

3. William King "Bill" Harvey was an American Central Intelligence Agency officer best known for his role in the terrorism and sabotage campaign known as Operation Mongoose. He was known as "America's James Bond," a tag given to him by Edward Lansdale.

4. William Cornelius Sullivan (May 12, 1912 – November 9, 1977) was an assistant director of the Federal Bureau of Investigation who was in charge of the agency's domestic intelligence operations from 1961 to 1971. Sullivan was forced out of the FBI at the end of September 1971 due to disagreements with FBI director J. Edgar Hoover.

Statement of Policy

1) The removal of the President [JFK] and the Attorney General [RFK] from their positions because of high treason has been determined.

2) By their contacts with top-level intelligence officials of the Soviet Union and the subsequent release by the President and the Attorney General of the highest level security material to a government that stands in direct opposition to the United States, these individuals cannot be permitted to occupy their official positions.

3) By treating with the enemy on the Cuban issue and actively blocking legitimate military actions against a Soviet Cuban armed enemy in close proximity to the United States, these individuals have endangered the people of the United States and permitted enemies of

this country to actively place atomic weapons within the reach of many American cities.

4) Removal by impeachment or other legal means is considered unfeasible and too protracted.

5) Therefore, an alternative solution has been found to effect this removal.

6) This removal is the result of a consensus between the carious concerned official agencies.

7) This operation, codenamed ZIPPER, was under the direction of James Angleton of the Agency, assisted by Robert Crowley and William Harvey, also of the Agency.

8) The government departments directly concerned consisted of:

   a. The Central Intelligence Agency

   b. The Federal Bureau of Investigation.

   c. The Joint Chiefs of staff

9) Other government agencies involved but not with specific knowledge were:

   a. The U.S. Department of the Treasury, Secret Service Division

   b. The National Security Agency.

   c., The Naval Security Group.

   d. INTERARMCO.

   e. The U.S. Department of State, Passport Division.

10) Following the removal of the President (JFK), the new President (LBJ), who had been fully briefed prior to the act, agreed "in the interest if national concerns" to appoint a special Commission chaired by the Chief Justice, for the purpose of "setting public concerns to rest." Mr. Angleton was in complete control of all evidence presented to this Committee and worked closely in conjunction with Mr. Sullivan of the FBI to ensure that nothing was brought before the Committee that it did not want to acknowledge.

11) As both the Vice President and the Director of the Federal Bureau of Investigation had been slated for replacement by the Kennedy faction, their support for this project was practically guaranteed from the outset.

12) The Vice President came to believe that an attempt would be made on his life at the same time and was greatly concerned for his own safety.

13) As the Vice President and the Director of the FBI were longtime neighbors and very friendly, the Director has repeatedly assured the President that he was not a target and that no shots were fired at him in Dallas.

14) The President (LBJ) has been reassured but is still considered very leery of any possible such actions being taken against himself or members of his personal family.

15) One of the primary goals of ZIPPER, the removal of the Attorney General, has been discussed repeatedly with the President by DCI, and the President has agreed to gradually force him out of his position. He has stated, however, that the popularity of the AG is such that his removal must be performed with care.

16) Representative Ford, R, of Michigan, a member of the Commission, is working closely with director Hoover and reports all incoming information directly to him.

17) Full cooperation with friendly media sources has ensured that public attention has been drawn to Oswald as the sole killer. The President feels strongly that any attempt to portray Oswald as a tool of the Soviets is liable to create "too high a level of international tension," which the President feels might lead to direct confrontation with the Soviet Union.

18) The President is not receptive to plans of the JCS, supported entirely by the Agency, to eradicate Castro and his Marxist government from Cuba. The President states that war almost occurred as a result of the last military attempt to dis-lodge the Cuban dictator, and he does not wish to replay that aspect of the enforcement of the Monroe Doctrine.

19) The President has indicated, however, that an escalation of U.S. military involvement in French Indochina is not unreasonable. Reports given to him by the Agency, as well as the JCS, have been well received.

20) The President's aide, Jenkins, has also supported this idea, and the Secretary of Defense has come down strongly in favor of it.

21) The President believes that his occupancy of the White House is due to the death of his predecessor and has a desperate desire to achieve a degree of legitimacy.

22) He has been advised that a war-time President is always assured of reelection (i.e., Wilson, Roosevelt) but only in the event that the war is prosecuted with Vigor and has attendant military successes.

23) On a related topic, the French President DeGaulle, while in Washington for the late President's funeral, held several conferences with the new President as well as other officials to include the Agency.

24) The General stated several times and with some asperity that he had been the object of a number of assassination attempts in the past, some going back to the war, and that he had grown tired of them. He stated that the OAS attempts to shoot him or bomb him had been known to members of the Agency who and, in at least one case, assisted the IAS assassins.

25) The General also stated that he was aware through French intelligence reports that the assassins of the President were French citizens.

26) Because it is viewed as vital that the French become involved in NATO and to assuage the concerns of the General, guarantees were given both by the President and the DCI that no further actions would be undertaken that could result in an assassination and further, that the United States would actively support French commercial interests in French Indochina in return for French cooperation with NATO.

27) The French President agreed to this but made several oblique threats to the President about his reactions in the event of future Agency "meddling" in French domestic and foreign policy.

28) The General was reassured repeatedly on these points and is now apparently in agreement with the United States' aims in Southeast Asia. He made several remarks about the trade-in opium in that area being extremely lucrative and stated that he had his own problems with narcotics traffic in the Mediterranean area.

29) It is not believed, and electronic surveillance of the President's lines of communication while in the United States does not support the possibility that he might have actual knowledge of any American involvement, or projected involvement, in this area.

30) Both the Agency and the President feel that the French President has "fired a shot across our bows" but that these issues have now become resolved. The President feels, however, that the French will have (sic) to be watched carefully in the future and that if American interests become established in French Indochina, we had best consider our own interests at that time.

31) In the matter of the Soviet Union, it is evident that they were initially concerned that the removal of Kennedy might be laid at their doorstep. As this was certainly one of the objectives of the Agency as well as the JCS, it has been necessary to repeatedly reassure their leadership that there would be no such intimations in the future and that in addition, there would be no further attempts to execute any military or overt clandestine operations against either Cuba, or its leader, Castro.

32) In the matter of the public perception of the Dallas action, extensive use has been made of Agency connections with major American media organs, i.e., the New York Times and the Washington Post. The Times is strongly supporting the Commission and its findings and we are assured that they will continue to do so. The same attitude has been clearly and strongly expressed by the Post.

Chapter 6

Zipper Meetings Compendium — March 1963 to December 1963

Reprinted from The Crowley Documents in Regicide

Summary of executive meetings and communications. Note: In most cases, the participants listed were in attendance. In some cases, not noted, one or more of the participants were absent but subsequently fully informed of salient material discussed or were involved by telephonic participation in meetings. In the following compendium, many meetings, conferences or telephonic communications are not fully covered.

Abbreviations used in the ZIPPER Document

DCI   Director of Central Intelligence, John McCone

DD/FBI   Deputy Director of Federal Bureau of Investigation, William Sullivan

USMC   United States Marine Corps JCS Joint Chiefs of Staff of U.S. Armed Forces

SIGINT   Signals Intelligence AG Attorney General, Robert F. Kennedy

OAS   Organisation de l'armée secrète, French Secret Army Organization

JJA   James Jesus Angleton, CIA Counterintelligence

RTC	Robert Trumbull Crowley, CIA Clandestine Operations
VP	Vice President, Lyndon B. Johnson
WKH	William King Harvey, senior official of the CIA
Met.Club	Metropolitan Club, Washington, D.C.
AF	Abe Fortas, advisor to Lyndon B. Johnson
SG	Sam Giancana, Chicago Mafia chief
U/C	Unione Corse, Corsican Mafia
SC	Sam Cummings, INTERARMCO (CIA proprietary) ARM unidentified Lancer
SS	Code name for Secret Service for J. F. Kennedy travels
NSA	National Security Agency
WJ	Walter Jenkins, advisor to Lyndon B. Johnson
AF1	Air Force One (President's official aircraft) UClub University Club, D.C.
MC	Marshal Carter, senior officer of CIA, later with NSA
D/NSA	Director NSA, Gordon Blake
BB	Binjamin Baumann, Shin Beth (Israel)
AWD	Allen Welsh Dulles, former DCI

This page its reprinted from Crowley's documents, noting the checkmarks of his copy:

Synopsis of executive meetings and communications.

Note:

    In most cases, the participants listed above were in attendance. In some cases, not noted, one or more of the participants were absent but subsequently fully informed of salient material discussed or were involved by telephonic participation in meetings.

    In the following compendium, many meetings, conferences or telephonic communications are not fully covered.

Summary of Conferences held March-November 1963

✓ 1 MAR 63

8:30 AM- Noon

    Conference with DCI, JJA, RTC. Implementation of ZIPPER. Presentation of RFK intercepts to DCI. Review of investigative data to date. DCI requests more data.

✓ 2 MAR 63

9:45 AM- 11:15 AM

    Presentation by JJA and RTC to DCI of evidentiary material.

2:20 PM

    Request by DCI for interview with Director/FBI.

4 MAR 63

8:15 AM-10:00 AM

    Conference with DCI, JJA with Director/FBI and DD/FBI Sullivan.

7 MAR 63

8:30 PM- 12:06 AM

    Conference with JJA and Sullivan.

1 MAR 63

8:30 AM-Noon

Conference with DCI, JJA, RTC. Implementation of ZIPPER. Presentation of RFK   intercepts   to   DCI. Review of investigative data to date. DCI requests more data.

2 MAR 63

9:45 AM - 11:15 AM

Presentation by JJA and RTC to DCI of evidentiary material.

2:20 PM

Request by DCI for an interview with the Director/FBI

4 MAR 63

8:15 AM - 10:00 AM

Conference with DCI, JJA, Director/FBI, DD/FBI Sullivan.

10:20 AM - 10: 35 AM

Conference with DCI, JJA, RTC, and Sullivan.

7 MAR 63

8:30 PM-12:06 AM

Conference with JJA and Sullivan

8 MAR 63

2:02 PM-3:45 PM

Conference with JJA, RTC in re RFK.

4:15 PM- 4:38 PM

Telephone conference JJA with DCI concerning the above meeting

12 MAR 63

8:30 AM-9:23 AM

Conference JJA and Sullivan

1:20 PM- 2:10 PM

Lunch conference with JJA and RTC. Joined by DCI.

13 MAR 63

9:10 AM- 9:30 AM

Telephone conference by DCI with Walter Jenkins in re VP. Request for personal interview.

3:30 PM- 3:34 PM

Conference JJA with DCI on Jenkin's request.

14 MAR 63

9:45 AM- 10:23 AM and 3:37 PM - 4:11 PM

Conferences with JJA, Jenkins, RTC and telephone conference with WKH on   ZIPPER. Views of the VP are discussed. Extreme caution on the part of the VP subject of both conferences. Tentative acceptance of the basic thrust of ZIPPER. VP to speak with DCI.

15 MAR 63

12:35 PM-1:43 PM

Luncheon conference with DCI Jenkins and A. Fortas, Met. Club. Present: JJA and   RTC. Discussion by VP's aides of two conversations with DIR/FBI Hoover on

ZIPPER. AF requests copies of telephone intercepts.

16 MAR 63

1:08 PM- 1:16 PM

Telephone conference by RTC with SG in re U/C.

1:24 PM- 2:19 PM

Telephone conference by RTC with JJA in re SG.

2:45 PM- 3:10 PM

Telephone conversation by JJA with DCI in re SG.

3:32 PM- 4:50 PM

Telephone conference with WKH by JJA in re SG.

18 MAR 63

8:44 AM- 9:29 AM

Telephone conference by JJA w SC/ INTERARMCO in re weaponry and delivery.

3:04 PM-3:30 PM

Telephone conferences with DCI and RTC in re SC analysis.

9:30 PM- 11: 27 PM

Conference RTC with WJ and AF. Copies of RFK reports for VP.

19 MAR 63

11:45 AM

Telephone report by SG to RTC concerning the need for US passports.

20 MAR 63

3:27 PM- 3:29 PM

Telephone conference by RTC with SG in re-passports. Affirmative response.

21 MAR 63

11:55 AM-2:37 PM

Lunch meeting with DCI, RTC, and JJA. Review of telephone taps on RFK. Report by JJA on Soviet receipts.

25 MAR 63

9:45 AM- 10:17 AM

Telephone conference with Jenkins in re VP, RTC

28 MAR 63

3:15 PM- 4:25 PM

Conference with DCI and JJA Coordination of JCS objectives with ZIPPER

4:45 PM-4:48 PM

Telephone conference with Jenkins concerning VP RTC

4:55 PM-5:01 PM

Telephone conference with DCI on VP RTC

29 MAR 63

2:35 PM-3:15 PM

Telephone conference: DCI with FBI/Sullivan

6:60 PM-9:55 PM

Conference with RTC and WKH reference logistics of ZIPPER

3 APRIL 63

11:08 PM- 1:21 AM

Telephone conference between JJA and Amos Minor, Israel l, in re possible   cooperation in ZIPPER

4 APRIL 63

11:31 AM- 1:02 PM

Conference with JJA and RTC in re Minor assistance.

3:35 PM-4:45 PM

Telephone conference RTC and SG, Sicilian referral.

9 APRIL 63

8:31 AM- 8:45 AM

Telephone conference, JJA with Lt COL Cass, S'Domingo in re ZIPPER —   Agreement for conference

9:08 AM- 9:14 AM

Conference with DCI and JJA concerning Cass meeting and SG progress

11 APRIL 63

1:45 PM- 1:56 PM

Telephone conference with Jenkins in re VP. Clarification of DCI memo.

2:30 PM-2:46 PM

Telephone conference with Pentagon in re Cass meeting.

4:36 PM - 5:15 PM

Meeting JJA and DCI on progress for Zipper. No direct contact between DCI and Cass.

13 APRIL 63

8:22 PM- 9:07 PM

Telephone conference RTC and SC in re ZIPPER

14 APRIL 63

9:35 AM-11:07 AM

Conference with DCI, JJA, WKH Reference update with WKH. Suggestion received from Lemnitzer on rep. Lt COL Cass in S'Domingo.

2:35 PM-3:12 PM

Telephone conference with LtCOL Cass in re ZIPPER

15 APRIL 63

12:35 AM-2:23 PM

Conference with WKH and SC concerning weaponry and logistics INTERARMCO

5:20 PM- 5:45 PM

Telephone conference with Jenkins in re VP

18 APRIL 63

1:23 PM- 1:25 PM

Telephone conference with SC of INTERARMCO

2:01 PM-2:05 PM

Telephone contact with SG in Chicago in re RTC meeting.
RTC

2:25 PM-2:31 PM

Telephone conference with JJA concerning SG.

2:33 PM- 2:40 PM

Meeting with DCI about Chicago. RTC, JJA

19 APRIL 63

Telephone conference with ARM in re LANCER SS protection.
JJA

23 APRIL 63

Conference with RTC and SG concerning logistics for ZIPPER.
Chicago

24 APRIL 63

Conference with RTC and SG concerning logistics for ZIPPER.
Chicago

3:09 PM- 3:33 PM Conference with JJA and LtCol Cass in re
ZIPPER

30 APRIL 63

9:31 AM -1:45 AM

Telephone conference with RTC and Jenkins in re VP.
Further clarification on post-   ZIPPER.

2:20 PM- 5:38 PM

Conference DCI and Sullivan in re contact with
Director/FBI. Supply RFK   transcripts.

2 MAY 63

1:00 PM- 2:59 PM

Conference with DCI, JJA, RTC, and Sullivan in re intercepted phone conversations from   Hickory Hill. Also, intercepted and decoded conversations from the Soviet embassy.

4:09 PM-4:21 PM

Telephone conversation between RTC and SG on Marseilles contacts.

4:30 PM- 5:37 PM

Conference with RTC and JJA concerning SG referrals. Also, Mass. sailboat plan.   Rejected.

5 MAY 63

2:02 PM- 4:45 PM

Telephone conference between JJA RTC. With reference to progress on   ZIPPER.

The subject of discussion:

1. SS Presidential security

2. Projected Presidential visits, a. Inside US. b. Outside the US

3. Disinformation in reports to the White House aimed at disrupting channels of communication.

4. Contact with NSA in re blocking of calls transmitting information to the Soviet Union

5. Close coordination with JCS concerning military action against Cuba

6. Ascertaining attitudes of VP in re para 5

7. Communicating compromising material on President to Soviet Union loss of confidence

8. Information on planned RFK prosecution of VP aides. To discredit the VP and give a motive for removing from the ticket in '64. Give to AF?

This entry is the most informative. It is obvious that this log was prepared by various people over the period from March through November. Vice President Lyndon Johnson obviously was brought into the plot through contact with Walter Jenkins and Abe Fortas. Not a bold man, Johnson's concerns are entirely typical of the man. He had forced himself on the 1960 Democratic ticket against Kennedy's wishes, and throughout the thousand days of the Kennedy presidency, Johnson was treated with contempt by Kennedy's people. Their favorite epithet was 'Uncle Cornpone,' and it became common knowledge that Kennedy was planning to replace Johnson on the 1964 ticket. To accomplish this, Bobby Kennedy was preparing criminal charges against Bobby Baker, one of Johnson's top aides. Johnson was aware that such charges would give the Kennedy faction the ability to force him off the ticket. Since Vice Presidents traditionally have run for the Presidency at the expiration of the mandatory two-term limit, any hope of gaining the White House would have been dashed. Johnson, therefore, became a willing, if very timid, participant in the ZIPPER project.

6 MAY 63

9:34 AM- 10:21 AM

Conference JJA with DCI in re 5 May conference. Approval noted.

11:10 AM-3:17 PM

Telephone conferences by JJA & RTC with:

a. WJ in re VP

b. JCS in re ZIPPER and plans

c. SG in re team progress

d. SC in re logistics.

The inclusion of the Joint Chiefs of Staff is a thread that runs throughout the entire development of ZIPPER. Giancana obviously reported on his efforts to line up a foreign team, and Sam Cummings, who was in charge of the weapons, reported on his task.

10 MAY 63

Lunch conference DCI, Sullivan, JJA, RTC, WKH Discussion of the progress of ZIPPER. The decision to launch a disinformation program in re Soviets. The decision to expand sources to
include source AF1 Decision for dual payments to UC and to SG

AF1 refers to Air Force One, but any attempt to destroy the President's aircraft was eventually abandoned due to extraordinary security in place. Both Giancana and the Unione Corse were to be paid for their services, the former to ensure his continued cooperation.

14 MAY 63

4:45 PM

Report by SC in re weaponry

21 MAY 63

3:20 PM- 4:11 PM

Conference DCI, RTC in re NSA communications surveillance

The National Security Agency or NSA is, and was in 1963, positioned to monitor all foreign and domestic telephone, and radio traffic. Subsequently, they have added the ability to intercept Internet and fax messages.

24 MAY 63

2:25 PM

Contact with source on AF1. It was at this point that any action involving the President's aircraft was abandoned.

3:10 PM

Conference DCI, JJA on subject payment for AF1 source

25 MAY 63

2:10 PM-4:43 PM

The conference, UClub, RTC, JJA, WKH with rep, Chair/JCS in re ZIPPER. Coordination of ZIPPER w. MARLINSTRIKE

The meaning of MARLINSPIKE is not known at this writing but appears to be a plan designed to draw the United States into war with Cuba, a strong desire of the JCS and its Chief, General Lyman Lemnitzer.

27 MAY 63

9:45 AM- 12:00 PM & 2:30 PM- 5:52 PM

Conference JJA, RTC in re ZIPPER

28 MAY 63

8:32 AM-9:01 AM

Telephone conference JJA with Lt COL Cass in re ZIPPER

11:34 AM- 12:30 PM

Conference JJA, DCI in re NSA transcripts

31 MAY 63

1:35 PM-2:50 PM

Conference JJA, AF in re VP Discussion of VP attitudes in re MARLINSTRIKE,   ZIPPER

3:00 PM-3:21 PM

Telephone conference JJA. JCS in re AF conference.

3:30 PM-3:34 PM

Telephone conference JJA DCI in re AF & JCS

3 JUNE 63

2:20 PM- 3:05 PM

Conference with DD Carter and GEN Blake, DIR/NSA, concerning   ZIPPER.

1. NSA SIGINT surveillance of Cuba, Mexico, and the Dominican Republic.

2. NSA domestic surveillance,

3. TASS communications.

4. Soviet internal communications

5. White House communications General Marshal Carter, USA, was a senior official in the CIA and later went on to head the NSA.

4 JUNE 63

Lunch conference, DD/MC, JJA, RTC in reference to Blake's position. Lieutenant General   Gordon Blake, USAF, was Director of the NSA from July 1962 through May 1965. He was replaced by General Marshal Carter.

6 JUNE 63

7:30 PM- 9:20 PM

Conference, JJA, RTC in re NSA intercepts.

11 JUNE 63

9:55 AM-10:02 AM

Telephone conference with AF in re VP Anxiety

12 JUNE 63

12:30 PM-12:45 PM

Telephone conference with LtCOL Cass, S'Domingo As U.S. Military Attaché to the   Dominican Republic, Lt. Colonel Cass had been involved with the CIA assassination of Trujillo and had handled the weapons used in the killing, which had arrived in the diplomatic pouch.

4:11 PM- 4:34 PM

Telephone conference with JJA & A. Manor in re UC team.

5:30 PM- 6:45 PM

Telephone conference with JJA & AF in re VP. More reassurances are needed.   True to form, Lyndon Johnson is still trying to have his cake and eat it as well.

19 JUNE 63

11:35 AM- 12:40 PM

Telephone conference, DD/MC with D/NSA Blake concerning NSA intercepts

1:45 PM-1:50 PM

The telephone conference, DD/MC with RTC concerning SG.

24 JUNE 63

5:39 PM-5:51 PM

The telephone conference, DCI and JJA, RTC and WKH Report from SC in re weapons.

25 JUNE 63

3:09 PM- 3:30 PM

Telephone conference, WKH with LtCOL Cass, S'Domingo. Receipt of NSA report

26 JUNE 63

9:30 AM- 9:54 AM

Telephone conference. AF to RFK in re VP. Agreement in general. At this point in time, Lyndon Johnson had decided to join the Presidential poker game.

10:07 AM- 10:09 AM

Telephone conference RTC with DCI. in re AF call

11:30 AM-11:45 AM

Telephone conference RTC with Lemnitzer aide in re ZIPPER

JULY

3 JULY 63

The arrival of B. Bauman from Toronto. Binjamin Bauman, a Shin Bet operative, had been a member of the terrorist Stern Gang and was one of the men who planted a huge bomb in the King David Hotel in Jerusalem in 1946. A large number of British officers and civilians were killed in the subsequent blast. Bauman was recruited by Angleton through his friend, Amos Manor, head of the Shin Bet, the internal security organ of the Israeli government.

4 JULY 63

7:39 PM- 11:45 PM

Receipt of courier reports NSA. Personal interview with JJA, RTC & MC with Bauman

5 JULY 63

2:33 PM-3:15 PM

Evaluation of AF1 material by JJA, WKH, and RTC. Conference with DCI, JJA on AF1 findings. Negative

11 JULY 63

11:00 AM- 12:15 PM

Conference with JJA, MC, and RTC in re-intercepts. Review by JJA on RFK and White House telephone transcripts. It is obvious that both James Angleton and NSA were involved in electronic surveillance of the Attorney General and in all probability, the White House as well.

16 JULY 63

10:45 AM- 11:14 AM

Telephone conference with MC and Blake in re NSA intercepts.

1:45 PM- 5:15 PM

Conference with BB, JJA MC in re ZIPPER and UC team.

17 JULY 63

6:30 PM-11:00 PM

Conference with JJA & BB

9:45 PM- 10:15 PM

Telephone conference JJA & BB with SC in re weapons

19 JULY 63

7:01 PM-11:43 PM

Conference with DCI, AWD, MC, JJA, and RTC in re ZIPPER. Agreement in principle on all issues.

AWD are the initials of Allen Welsh Dulles, former longtime head of the CIA who had been fired by Kennedy over the CIA failures in the Bay of Pigs fiasco.

31 JULY 63

9:40 AM-10:20 AM

Telephone conference with CHAIR/JCS in re AWD, VP overviews.

11:30 AM-1:29 PM

Conference, MC, JJA, RTC in re ZIPPER. Transfer operation to WKH

It is at this point that the actual execution of ZIPPER was turned over to William King Harvey. All future records reflect a series of progress reports by Harvey on a weekly basis to his superiors.

9 AUGUST 63

   1:50 PM-2:10 PM Conference, WKH, JJA Progress Report

16 AUGUST 63

   7:50 PM-11:01 PM

      Conference, WKH, JJA Progress Report

23 AUGUST 63

   8:15 PM-10:19 PM

      Conference, WKH, JJA RTC Progress Report

30 AUGUST 63

   7:50 PM- 8:45 PM

      Conference, WKH, JJA Progress Report

6 SEPT 63

   3:19 PM-5:12 PM

      Conference, WKH, MC, JJA Progress Report

12 SEPT 63

   2:45 PM- 3:18 PM

      Conference, WKH, JJA Progress Report

20 SEPT 63

10:20 PM- 1:45 AM

Conference, WKH, RTC MC Progress Report

27 SEPT 63

9:30 AM-10:17 AM

Conference, WKH, DCI, MC, JJA, RTC Progress Report

18 OCT 63

7:45 PM- 11:30 PM

Conference, WKH, JJA Progress Report Dallas

This is the only reference in this document to Dallas, Texas. On the 17th of October, Lee Harvey Oswald began his employment at the Texas Book Depository.

24 OCT 63

11:20 AM- 11:22 AM

Telephone conference, SG, JJA in re UC arrival Montreal. At this point, members of the Corsican assassination team arrived in Quebec, Canada.

1 NOV 63

8:40 PM-12: PM

Conference WKH, WTC Progress Report

14 NOV 63

1:45 PM-1:56 PM

Telephone conference, WKH MC. in re UC/Dallas The Unione Corse team was now in Dallas and preparing for their task when President Kennedy made his official visit on November 22.

Chapter 7

The Hoover Memorandum

Reprinted from The Crowley Documents in Regicide

UNITED STATES DEPARTMENT OF JUSTICE

FEDERAL BUREAU OF INVESTIGATION

Washington, D.C.

1:39 p.m.

November 29, 1963

Memorandum for:

- Mr. Tolsen

- Mr. Belmont

- Mr. Mohr

- Mr. Conread

- Mr. DeLoach

- Mr. Evans

- Mr. Rosen

- Mr. Sullivan

The President [LBJ] called an asked if I am familiar with the proposed group. They are trying to get to study my report - two from the house, two from the Senate, two from the courts, and a couple of outsiders. I replied that I had not heard of that but had seen reports from the Senate Investigating Committee.

The President stated he wanted to get by just with my file and my report. I told him I thought it would be very bad to have a rash of investigations. He then indicated the only way to stop it is to appoint a high-level committee to evaluate my report and tell the house and Senate not to go ahead with the investigation. I stated that it would be a three-ring circus.

The president then asked what I think about Allen Dulles, and I replied that he is a good man. He then asked me about John McCloy, and I stated I am not as enthusiastic about McCloy, that he is a good man but I am not so certain as to the matter of publicity he might want. The President then mentioned General Norstad, and I said he is a good man. He said in the House he might try Boggs and Ford and in the Senate Russell and Cooper, and he indicated Cooper of Kentucky, whom he described as a judicial man, stating he would not want Javits. I agree on this point. He then reiterated Ford of Michigan, and I indicated I knew of him but did not know him and had never seen him except on television the other day and that he handled himself well on television.

The President then mentioned that Jenkins had told him that I had designated Mr. DeLoach to work with them as he had on the Hill. He indicated they appreciated that and just wanted to tell me they considered Mr. DeLoach as high class as I do and that they salute me for knowing how to pick good men.

I advised the President that we hope to have the investigation wrapped up today but probably won't have it before the first of the week as an angle in Mexico is giving us trouble — the matter of Oswald's getting

$6400 from the Cuban Embassy and coming back to this country with it that we are not able to prove that fact, that we have the information he was there on September 18 and we are able to prove he was in New Orleans on that date, that a story came in changing the date to September 28 and he was in Mexico on the 28th. I related that the police have again arrested Duran, a member of the Cuban Embassy, that they will hold her for two to three days, will confront her with the original informant, and will also try a lie detector test on her. The President then inquired if I pay attention to the lie detector test., I answered that I would not pay 100% attention to them, that it was only a psychological asset tin the investigation, and that I would not want to be a part of sending a man to the chair on a lie detector test. I explained that we have used them in bank investigations, and a person will confess before the lie detector test is finished, more or less fearful it will show him guilty. I said the lie detector test has this psychological advantage. I further stated that it is a misnomer to call it a lie detector since the evaluation of the char made by the machine is made by a human being, and any human being is apt to make the wrong interpretation.

I stated if Oswald had lived and had taken a lie detector test, this, with the evidence we have, would have added that much strength to the case, that there is no question he is the man.

I also told him that Rubenstein down there has offered to take a lie detector test, but his lawyer must be consulted first, that I doubt the lawyer will allow him to do so that he has a west coast lawyer somewhat like the Edward Bennett Williams type and almost as much of a shyster.

The President asked if we have any relationship between the two as yet. I replied that at the present time we have not, that there was a story that the fellow had been in Rubenstein's nightclub that it has not been confirmed. I told the President that Rubenstein is a very seedy character had a bad record — street brawls, fights, etc.; that in Dallas, if a fellow came into his nightclub and could not pay his bill completely, Rubenstein would beat him up and throw him out, that he did not drink or smoke that he was an egomaniac; that he likes to be in the limelight; knew all of the police officers in the white light district; let them come in and get food an liquor, etc. and that is how I think he got into police headquarters. I said if they made any move, the pictures did not show it even when they saw him approach and he got right up to Oswald and pressed the pistol against Oswald's stomach, that neither officer on either side made any effort to grab Rubenstein — not until after the pistol was fired. I said, secondly, the chief of police admits he moved Oswald in the morning as a convenience and at the request of motion picture people who wanted daylight. I said insofar as trying Rubenstein and Oswald together; we have not yet done so, that there are a number of stories that tied Oswald to the Civil Liberties Union in New York in which he applied for membership and the Fair Play for Cuba Committee, which is pro-Castro, directed by communists and financed to some extent by the Castro Government.

The President asked how many shots were fired, and I told him three. He then asked me if any were fired at him. I said no that three shots were fired at the President, and we have them. I stated that our ballistic experts were able to prove the shots were fired by this guy, that the President was hit by the first and third bullets and the second hit the Governor, that there were three shots, that one complete bullet rolled out of the President's head; that it tore a large part of the President's head off; that in trying to massage his heart on the way into the hospital they loosened the bullet which fell on the stretcher and we have that.

He then asked where they aimed at the President. I replied they were aimed at the President, no question about that.

I further advised him that we had also tested the fact you could fire those three shots in three seconds. I explained that there is a story out that there must have been more than one man to fire several shots, but we have proven it could be done by one man.

The President then asked how it happened that Connally was hit. I explained that Connally turned to the President when the first shot was fired and that, in turn, he got hit. The President then asked, if Connally had not been in his seat, would the President have been hit by the second shot? I said yes.

I related that on the fifth floor of the building where we found the wrapping paper, we found three empty shells that had been fired and one that had not been fired; he had four but didn't fire the fourth, which threw the guy aside; went down the steps, was seen by a police officer, the manager told the officer that Oswald was all right, worked there; they let him go; he got on a bus; went to his home and got a jacket; then came back downtown; walking; the police officer who was killed stopped him, not knowing who he was; and he fired and killed the police officer.

The President asked if we can prove that and I answered yes. I further related that Oswald then walked another two blocks went to the theater; the woman selling tickets was suspicious — said he was carrying a gun when he went into the theater — that she notified the police; the police and our man went in and located Oswald. I told him they had quite a struggle with Oswald but that he was subdued and shown out and taken to police headquarters.

I advised the President that apparently, Oswald had come down the steps form the fifth floor; that, apparently the elevator was not used.

The President then indicated our conclusions are: (1) he is the one who did it; (2) after the President was hit, Governor Connally was hit; (3) the President would have been hit three times except for the fact that Governor Connally turned after the first show and was hit by the second; (4) whether he was connected with the Cuban operation with money we are trying to nail down. I told him that is what we were trying to nail down, that we have copies of correspondence, that none of the letters dealt with any indication of violence or assassination, and that they were dealing with a visa to go back to Russia.

I advised the President that his wife had been very hostile, would not cooperate, and speaks only Russian; that yesterday, who said, if we could give assurance she would be allowed to remain in the country, she would cooperate; and that I told our agents to give that assurance and sent a Russian speaking agent to Dallas last night to interview her. I said I do not know whether or not she has any information but we would learn what we could. The President asked how Oswald had access to the fifth floor of the building. I replied that he had access to all floors. The President asked where his office was, and I stated he did not have any particular place, that he was not situated in any particular place, that he was just a general packer of requisitions that came in for books form Dallas schools, that he would have had proper access to the fifth and sixth floors whereas usually the employees were down on lower floors. The President then inquired if anybody saw him on the fifth floor, and I stated he was seen by one of the workmen before the assassination.

The President then asked if we got a picture taken of him shooting the gun, and I said no. He asked what was the picture sold for $25,000, and I advised im this was a picture of the parade showing Mrs. Kennedy crawling out of the back seat that there was no Secret Service Agent on the back of the car' that in the past they have added steps on the back of the car and usually had an agent on either side standing on the bumper' that I did no know why this was not done - that the President may have requested it' that the bubble top was not up but I understand the bubble top was not worth anything because it was made entirely of plastic; that I had learned much to my surprise that the Secret Service does not have any armored cars.

The President asked if I have a bulletproof car and I told him I most certainly have. I told him we use it here for my own use and, whenever we have any raids, we make use of the bulletproof car on them. I explained that it is a limousine that has been armor-plated and that it looks exactly like any other car. I stated I think the President ought to have a bulletproof car that, from all I understand, the Secret Service has had two cars with metal plates underneath the car to take care of hand grenades or bombs thrown out on the street. I said this is European, that there have been several such attempts on DeGaulle's life, but they do not do that in this country, that all assassinations have been done with guns, and for that reason, I think very definitely the President ought to always ride in a bulletproof car; that it certainly would prevent anything like this ever happening again but that I do not mean a sniper could not snipe him from a window if he were exposed.

The President asked if I meant on his ranch; he should be in a bulletproof car. I said I would think so that the little car we rode around in when I was at the ranch should be bulletproofed' that it ought to be done very quietly. I told him we have four bullet proof cars in the Bureau: one on the West Coast, one in New York, and two here. I said this could be done quietly without publicity and without pictures taken of it if handled properly, and I think he should have one on his ranch.

The President then asked if I think all the entrances should be guarded. I replied, by all means, that he had almost to be in the capacity of a so-called prisoner because, without that security, anything could be done. I told him lots of phone calls had been received over the last four or five days about threats on his life' that I talked to the Attorney General about the funeral procession from the White House to the Cathedral, and that I was opposed to it. The President remarked that the Secret Service told them not to but the family wanted to do it. I stated that was what the Attorney General told me, but I was very much opposed to it. I further related that I saw the procession from the Capitol to the White House on Pennsylvania and while they had police standing on the curbs, when the parade came, the police turned around and looked at the parade.

The President then stated he is going to take every precaution he can; that he wants to talk to me; and asked if I would put down my thoughts. He stated I was more than head of the FBI - I was his brother and personal friend' that he knew I did not want anything to happen to his family' that he has more confidence in me than anybody in town' and that he would not embroil me in a jurisdictional dispute but that he did want to have my thoughts on the matter to advocate as his own opinion. I stated I would be glad to do this for him and that I would do anything I could. The President expressed his appreciation.

Very truly yours

/s/J.E.H

John Edgar Hoover

Director

Silence The Witnesses

Many books and websites list people who were murdered to silence their knowledge of the JFK assassination. Sadly, this is what has transfixed my attention, imagining I could have been one of them. My heart bleeds for these people. Some knew they were playing with fire. Others had no clue. Rest in peace. ~J. Manning

J. Edgar Hoover, under orders of President Lyndon B. Johnson, gave the go-ahead to the CIA to kill "troublemaker witnesses."

Excerpt from Crowley memo:

JJA: I spoke with Hoover about this and as a good, personal friend of the President, has agreed to mollify him and put his irrational fears to rest. Hoover has advised the President that certain "negative forces" are at work against those agencies who wish to protect and support the President.

The President has urged Hoover to find a way to "convince " these "troublemakers" to cease their negative remarks "in the best interests" of the nation"

This gives us the opportunity of silencing anyone who might express dangerous opinions about Dallas. ~Crow

Mary Pinchot Meyer

On October 12, 1964, shortly after noon, Mary Pinchot Meyer, 44, former wife of Cord Meyer, Jr., a senior CIA official, was found shot to death in a wooded area near her Georgetown studio. She had been shot once in the head and once in the upper body, a professional technique of assassination.

A dazed black day laborer was found in the vicinity by police, and although not matching the description of an eyewitness, he was arrested and put on trial for murder. A large number of CIA personnel were present immediately after the discovery of the body. The suspect, Ray Crump, had no coherent statement for the police, and a search of the area failed to locate the handgun used in the killing. He was waiting on a street corner for day labor before being found on the towpath near Mary Meyer's body. The prosecution depicted him as a rapist, but he had no record of such offenses. Crump was acquitted at his subsequent trial.

Mary Meyer's husband, Cord Meyer, Jr., was a close personal friend of James Angleton and a very bitter enemy of John Kennedy. Cord Meyer's intense hatred of Kennedy stemmed from his former wife, Mary, being Kennedy's long-term mistress after their divorce. Mary Meyer introduced LSD to the President during her many visits to the White House. Immediately after her murder, Crowley associate James Angleton was caught in her Georgetown studio going through her papers. He later removed her diary and kept it. Robert Crowley, who saw it, stated it contained a significant number of references to her connection with Kennedy, including the use of drugs at White House sex parties and blaming the CIA for the death of her lover the year before. She made indiscreet comments on her suspicions of CIA involvement in the Kennedy killing to a number of her neighbors, a significant number of whom had husbands who were senior CIA officials. Mary Meyer's murder is still unsolved, and the police records have disappeared. Shortly after her murder, Cord Meyer painted "Tough Luck, Mary" on the Key Bridge near the site of her death.

Lee Harvey Oswald

John Curington, the former right-hand man to oil billionaire H.L. Hunt, reported that in the middle of the night after the JFK murder, Hunt asked him to fetch his friend, Joe Civello, the head of the mafia in Dallas, at his restaurant and to come to his house. No phone calls. Hunt wanted Civello to give Jack Ruby $50,000 to kill Oswald, fearing Oswald would talk. Oswald was shot dead by Jack Ruby two days later, on November 24, 1963, at 24 years old. With all the planning by the CIA to set-up witnesses for the Oswald trial, his murder may not have been part of the carefully implemented CIA plan of many moving parts.

Chapter 8

The Beneficiaries of the JFK Murder

Texas Oil Barons

Oil tycoon H.L. Hunt, the wealthiest man in the world at that time, was part of a group of 25 oil barons and business people who were friends, met for coffee at shops in Dallas in the mornings, and socialized together at their clubs. They were doing all kinds of deals around the country with the mafia. They financed the CIA, who allegedly recruited Mob bosses Sam Giancana and Santo Trafficante to mobilize other mobsters to assassinate Fidel Castro in 1961, called Operation Mongoose.

By 1963, Kennedy wanted to abolish the 27-and-a-half percent oil depletion allowance. This would have cost the oil barons hundreds of millions of dollars, so they vehemently hated the Kennedys. Kennedy's death allowed the oil depletion allowance to stay at 27.5 percent. It remained unchanged during the Johnson presidency, saving the American oil industry $100 million. When Johnson left office, it dropped to 15 percent.

Is it possible that Clint Murchison, another oil magnate, also helped to fund the JFK assassination? Murchison was a close friend of both Lyndon Johnson and J. Edgar Hoover. His relationship with LBJ dates back to the 1948 Senate election. Murchison was one of his most prominent financial backers. Texas oil millionaires like Murchison fought hard to maintain its tax concessions. The most important was the oil depletion allowance, which allowed producers to deduct just 5 percent of their income, and the deduction was limited to the original cost of their property. However, in 1926, the depletion allowance increased to 27.5 percent. The oil barons knew losing their millions would be averted by LBJ becoming President by default.

When JFK was slaughtered, Russia's Khrushchev was in tears, fearing nuclear war. And Cuba's Castro feared a US invasion and gave an impressive speech the next day deconstructing the CIA's deception provocation for war.

Meanwhile, Clint Murchison's family maid, May Newman, describes the scene at Murchison's home: "The mood was very joyous and happy. For a whole week after, champagne and caviar flowed every day of the week. But I was the only one in that household at that time that felt any grief for his assassination." [The Men Who Killed Kennedy, The Guilty Men, Episode 9]

In my quest to do this research over 50 years, I used to think of myself as being on a jury at trial. In giving her testimony, Irish maid May Newman, by how she talked and mentioned things, like when some thought would pop into her head, she noted that—so everybody put much stock in what she said. Her intent and believability were better than the hundreds of people I profiled.

Author Russ Baker says Lyndon Johnson shared enmity toward Kennedy in the prevailing oil belt. He was the one person in the White House the oil company executives trusted. After Johnson ascended to the presidency, LBJ and newly elected Congressman Bush were often allies on such issues as the oil depletion allowance and the war in Vietnam. Oil executive Jack Crichton was close with Bush and head of a secretive Dallas-based, oil-connected military intelligence unit deeply immersed in aspects of the tragic events of November 22,

1963. Crichton was so plugged into the Dallas power structure that one of his company directors was Clint Murchison Sr., king of the oil depletion allowance, and another was D. Harold Byrd, owner of the Texas School Book Depository building.

Lyndon B. Johnson

Yet, even with all that *trust*, Lyndon Johnson still blamed the oil barons for the JFK murder. If LBJ did not become President, he would face an indictment. Clint Murchison was a close friend of both Lyndon Johnson and J. Edgar Hoover. His relationship with LBJ dates back to the 1948 Senate election. Murchison was one of his largest financial backers. Texas oil millionaires like Murchison fought hard to maintain its tax concessions. The most important of these was the oil depletion allowance., which allowed producers to deduct just 5 percent of their income, and the deduction was limited to the original cost of their property. However, in 1926, the depletion allowance increased to 27.5 percent.

Bobby Baker was the American political advisor to LBJ and an organizer for the Democratic Party. He became the Senate's Secretary to the Majority Leader. In 1963, he resigned during an investigation by the Democratic-controlled Senate into his business and political activities. The investigation included allegations of bribery and arranging sexual favors in exchange for Congressional votes and government contracts. The Senate investigation looked into the financial activities of Baker and Lyndon Johnson during the 1950s and was dropped after President Kennedy's assassination and Johnson's ascension to the presidency.

CIA: Allen Dulles, Richard Bissell, Charles Carbell

Allen Dulles, the first civilian Director of Central Intelligence (DCI), and his entourage, including Deputy Director for Plans Richard M. Bissell Jr. and Deputy Director Charles Cabell, were forced to resign. The three top guys got fired from the CIA by Kennedy. They were getting away with serving their interests under Truman and Eisenhower. After the Bay of Pigs fiasco, President Kennedy felt that the CIA was trying to not only treat him like a fool but also as a puppet on strings. Kennedy wasn't having any of that and wouldn't let Dulles get away with anything. JFK famously described his desire to "splinter the CIA into a thousand pieces and scatter it into the winds" after the disastrous Bay of Pigs invasion of Cuba.

At that time, the State Department proposed that the CIA be stripped of its covert action capacity and renamed. This move would have prevented Kennedy's murder.

However, Kennedy appointed John McCone, who took almost all the copies of the damning Bay of Pigs report, written by the Agency's inspector general, and burned them to ashes. The CIA had a legitimate Cold War mission in Europe and the Soviet Union, but they wanted an empire built within a government agency.

After Kennedy's assassination, Harry Truman wrote a newspaper column, more fully recited here, explaining that "I never had any thought that when I set up the CIA that it would be injected into peacetime cloak and dagger operations. ... I, therefore, would like to see the CIA be restored to its original assignment as the intelligence arm of the President... and that its operational duties be terminated or properly used elsewhere."

Truman revealed a great deal about his motives in founding the CIA and his aims in having the Agency provide intelligence briefings to the new president-elect, Gen. Dwight Eisenhower. The President reminisced about how there had been no CIA when he succeeded to the presidency in 1945.

At that time, by many accounts, he had been surprised to discover how much information relating to intelligence and national security matters had been withheld from him. The most dramatic evidence of how ill-informed he was came on his 12th day in office when Secretary of War Henry Stimson briefed him for the first time on the Manhattan (atomic bomb) Project. Truman also recalled how difficult it had been for him to obtain information from the various government departments, each of which seemed walled off from the others.

The Joint Chiefs of Staff

The Joint Chiefs of Staff consists of a chairman (CJCS), a vice chairman (VJCS), the chiefs of the Army, Marine Corps, Navy, Air Force, the chief of the National Guard Bureau, and today, the Chief of the Space Force. Keep in mind, during the Kennedy administration, these generals had to give their approval before the JFK assassination.

After the Bay of Pigs fiasco, the Joint Chiefs had already pitched Kennedy an idea that they were fully behind to execute an all-out nuclear first strike on the Soviet Union before the Soviet Union had completed their own all-out first strike capability.

The Joint Chiefs wanted to escalate the war in Vietnam and increase the defense budget greatly. President Eisenhower had kept them on a tight rein for eight years, and they wanted to expand. The Joint Chiefs had hoped to run roughshod over JFK. The Bay of Pigs and Cuba, in general, were not going the way that the CIA wanted, but they saw a new playground opening in Vietnam and were pushing hard to increase their operations there. Kennedy was having none of it.

Maxwell Davenport Taylor, born and raised in Missouri, served as the fifth chairman of the Joint Chiefs of Staff, appointed by President John F. Kennedy, after his assessment that Taylor wasn't a lunatic.

Chapter 9

A Convention of Hitmen in Dallas

Based on the definitive Warren Commission Report, if Oswald was the lone shooter, why did 20 professional hitmen, and perhaps more, all convene in Dallas on November 22, 1963? Some were perhaps invited by the mafia, some rogue hitmen, some were back-up, and some were plants set-up for the Oswald murder trial of JFK that never happened.

Malcolm Wallace -- LBJ's Personal Hit Man

Malcolm (Mac) Wallace was born to a farming family in Mount Pleasant, Texas, in October 1921. They moved to Dallas, and in 1939, Wallace joined the U.S. Marines. Wallace served on the aircraft carrier USS Lexington in Hawaii.

Malcolm Wallace was medically discharged from the U.S. Marines due to a fall off a ladder that badly injured his back. In September 1940, Wallace became a student at the University of Texas in Austin and was elected President of the Student Union. He became politically active when, in October 1944, Homer P. Rainey, President of the university and an outspoken supporter of the American Socialist Party, was fired. Wallace led a protest march of 8,000 students. Yet the campaign to have Rainey reinstated was unsuccessful. Clashes started when several members of the Board pressured Rainey to fire four professors of economics who espoused New Deal views.

Wallace graduated in June 1947 and married Mary DuBose Barton, the daughter of a Methodist preacher. While working on his doctorate at Columbia University and teaching, Edward Clark, a Texas lawyer and diplomat, introduced Wallace to Lyndon B. Johnson. Wallace began working with the United States Department of Agriculture in Texas in October 1950.

Wallace had an affair with LBJ's sister, Josefa Johnson. Josefa was also sleeping with John Kinser, the owner of a golf course in Austin. Josefa was known for her wild behavior. The affair with Wallace turned into a crime of passion. Kinser used Josefa to influence a loan from her powerful brother. LBJ refused, interpreting that Kinser was making a blackmail threat. Wallace caught wind of this, showed up at Kinser's mini-golf course, and shot him dead. Wallace was charged with murder but was released on bail after Edward Clark arranged for two of Johnson's financial supporters, M. E. Ruby and Bill Carroll, to post bonds on Wallace's behalf.

The power of law? Or the power of politicians?

LBJ's attorney, John Cofer, also agreed to represent Wallace. Cofer admitted his client's guilt but claimed it was an act of revenge as Kinser had been sleeping with Wallace's wife, the preacher's daughter. The jury found Wallace guilty of murder with malice, and 11 of the 12 jurors wanted the death penalty. Judge Charles O. Betts overruled the jury and announced a sentence of five years imprisonment. Then, Judge Betts suspended the sentence, and Wallace was immediately set free. Lyndon B. Johnson arranged a job for Wallace with the Luscombe Aircraft Corporation. LBJ wielded his power against the jury's decision to meet his ends.

LBJ - Estes Scam

Billie Sol Estes started a company providing irrigation pumps for farmers using cheap natural gas to replace pumps powered by electricity. Estes also sold anhydrous ammonia as a fertilizer. It was a great success, and Estes soon became a wealthy businessman. In 1953, the United States Junior Chamber of Commerce named him one of America's ten outstanding young men.

In 1958, Estes contacted Lyndon B. Johnson regarding subsidies. Over the next few years, Estes ran a vast scam to get federal agricultural subsidies for "growing" and "storing" non-existent cotton crops, totaling $21 million a year.

Henry Marshall was a clerk with the Agricultural Adjustment Administration and discovered this cotton allotment scam organized by Estes. Marshall sent a report to Washington to strengthen regulations to support the government's disapproval of this scam. However, Marshall was *ordered* to approve 138 cotton allotment transfers. As a result of sending the report of his findings to Washington, Marshall was offered a new post at headquarters. Disturbed, he considered it a bribe and refused the offer.

LBJ was afraid his role in this scam would become public knowledge. So LBJ gave the hit job to Mac Wallace. Days later, Marshall was found dead on his farm, shot five times with his rifle.

Wallace's initial plan was to kill Marshall by carbon monoxide poisoning, making it appear like a suicide. But Marshall caught Wallace in the act, and Marshall fought back, so Wallace used Marshall's gun to kill him. Now, LBJ had to use his influence with the authorities in Texas to cover up the botched murder.

Roger Stone, author of the 2013 book *The Man Who Killed Kennedy: The Case Against LBJ*, **called Wallace "Lyndon Johnson's personal hit man"** and also said that Wallace shot Kennedy from the sixth floor of the Texas School Book Depository. XX https://en.wikipedia.org/wiki/Malcolm_Wallace

Wallace went to work for Harry Lewis and L & G Oil. Barr McClellan claimed that the killing of Kennedy was paid for by oil millionaires such as Clint Murchison and Haroldson L. Hunt.

Kennedy's death allowed the oil depletion allowance to be 27.5 percent. It remained unchanged during the Johnson presidency, saving the American oil industry $100 million. When Johnson left office, it dropped to 15 percent.

In 1970, Wallace returned to Dallas and began pressing Edward Clark for more money for his part in the assassination of John F. Kennedy. According to author Barr McClellan, Clark decided Wallace had to be eliminated. After driving to see his daughter in Troup, Texas, Clark visited L & G's offices in Longview, Texas. Part of Wallace's exhaust pipe was rigged to flow into his car. On January 7, 1971, Malcolm Wallace appeared to have fallen asleep while driving to Pittsburg, Texas, crashing his car and dying of massive head injuries.

James Files

James Files (Sutton) was born in Alabama in January 1942. His family moved to Chicago, where he lived until joining the United States Army and serving with the 82nd Airborne in Vietnam (1959-60). After leaving the army, he met Charlie Nicoletti, a leading figure in the Chicago Mafia. Files was involved in the Bay of Pigs invasion.

In 1962, Files claims that he met Lee Harvey Oswald in Clinton, Louisiana.

In 1963, Files was recruited by Nicoletti to take part in the killing of John F. Kennedy. Nicoletti said the assassination was being organized by Sam Giancana, Johnny Roselli, and David Atlee Phillips. Files claimed Lee Harvey Oswald was involved in the plot, and his role was to plant the Mannlicher Rifle and shells in the Texas Book Depository.

On November 22, 1963, Files said he drove to Fort Worth, where he met Johnny Roselli, Jack Ruby, and Jim Brading. Ruby handed Rosselli an envelope that contained Secret Service identifications and an updated motorcade route map of Dallas.

Files and Nicoletti went to Dealey Plaza at about 10 a.m. Files agreed to use his Remington Fireball gun from behind the fence on the Grassy Knoll, and Nicoletti would position himself in the Dal-Tex Building. Files believed that Nicoletti's bullets hit both John F. Kennedy and John Connally. However, Files claimed it was his bullet that struck Kennedy in the head. Allegedly, Files got $30,000 for his role in the assassination. Files worked for Charlie Nicoletti until Nicoletti's murder on March 29, 1977.

Files was arrested on August 5, 1991, and charged with attempting to kill policeman David Ostertag. Files was sentenced to 30 years in Stateville Prison in Illinois and released in 2022.

In 1994, Files told his story to Joe West, and Bob Vernon took over the project on video, *The Murder of JFK: Confession of an Assassin* (1996). His confession was debunked by Edward Jay Epstein and private detective Jules Kroll, established from telephone records that Files was in Chicago, not Dallas, on November 22, 1963.

John R. Stockwell points out it was doubtful that the Mafia would still be planning the assassination of John F. Kennedy on the morning of November 22, 1963.

Before the Vietnam War, Files went to Laos to kill people for the CIA and clean house. Once back in Chicago, he became an excellent stock car driver and frequented demolition derbies, a mafia hangout. So, he got picked up by the mob in Chicago to be a driver for the big shots. If something was going on where they needed a fast driver to get away, Files was the guy.

A private detective was trying to find out what really happened to JFK. An FBI agent friend said to him, look up this guy James Files, and you didn't hear it from me.

So he finds Files in prison in Illinois, writes to him several times, and sends him a few dollars for his canteen. He asks Files if I can come up there can we talk for a while. He says no. Then he says yes. Then they become good friends.

The day before the assassination, Nicoletti says to Files, look, you know, the shots are good all, but if there is a miss, would you want to be in a place where you could guarantee the thing? Files say, sure, "Whatever you want me to do." So he was behind the wooden fence and made the shot that hit JFK in the head.

Yet, I don't believe it.

Jim Marrs, who wrote Crossfire, is the best researcher on JFK. He says he can't get Files out of his head. When Files tells his story, there are details about the hotel or motel he was in, the diner he ate at, and the names of the people there. It's hard not to believe somebody when you get all that specific information. He still claims that he did it. But see, they can't arrest them. Because the government says Files didn't do it. Oswald did it. So Files will never get caught.

David Sanchez Morales

Morales was one of the biggest killers for the CIA. He was a full-time agent and was in Dealey Plaza that day. The parade was turning from Houston Street onto Elm Street, where the car had to slow down. Morales was not there as a killer; he was one of the managers of the whole operation, for which he was famous. Yet he was so brutal that even those who worked with him feared him.

Morales was also involved in the Watergate Hotel scandal. Yet his two sons alleged that their father cut the information from his memoirs, *"American Spy: My Secret History in the CIA, Watergate, and Beyond,"* to avoid possible perjury charges.

Morales was recruited into Army Intelligence in 1947 and became an employee of the CIA in 1951 while retaining his Army cover. In 1952, he joined the Directorate for Plans, an organization instructed to conduct covert anti-Communist operations around the world.

In 1953, he returned to the United States, became involved in CIA's Black Operations, and moved to Cuba in 1958 to help support the government of Fulgencio Batista. Morales was a bully and a drinker and big enough to get away with a lot of stuff other people couldn't get away with." After a heavy drinking session at a local bar, Morales began boasting about the CIA's secret operations in Guantanamo Bay. Former CIA agent Edwin Wilson also credits Morales with the capture of Guevara. "He was a hard-drinking SOB, but he was the best operator the Agency ever had; he was at the top of the list. As a matter of policy, if the US government needed

80

someone or something neutralized, Dave would do it, including things repugnant to many people." He employed people he had been working with in Miami to undermine the government of Cuba, including figures in the anti-Castro Cuban community. It also involved American military advisers to groups like Alpha 66.

The Cubans believed the reason for this plot was that after the assassination of JFK, LBJ would order the invasion of Cuba.

Yet this was never the objective.

It was part of the overall conspiracy to keep Castro in power.

The presence of a communist state so close to the United States helped to reinforce the communist threat and the need for massive arms spending.

Morales was known to hate both Kennedys. A candid admission by Morales's childhood friend, Ruben Carbajal, said Morales was probably involved in both assassinations. Another witness put David Morales inside the Ambassador Hotel in Los Angeles on the night of June 5, 1968, during RFK's assassination.

When visiting Morale's home, his friend Robert Walton asked, "Why do you need so much security? You're thirty miles from the Mexican border." Morales replied, "I'm not worried about those people. I'm worried about my own."

Soon after Morales left the CIA, he made regular trips to Washington. Morales made his last trip there in early May 1978. When he got into town, Ruben Carbajal had a drink with Morales and told him he looked lousy. Morales said, "I don't know what's wrong with me. Ever since I left Washington, I feel like crap." That night, he went to the hospital.

Carbajal went to visit him in the morning, and deputy sheriffs surrounded his hospital room. Carbajal presumed, with all of Morales's drunk talk, he may have suffered a CIA-induced heart attack to silence him. Later that day (May 8, 1978), Morales's wife Joanne withdrew his life support and requested there should be no autopsy.

Charles Nicoletti

Connected to Sam Giancana, Morales, and Files

Charles Nicoletti was a leading figure in the Chicago Mafia. Working under Tony Accardo and Sam Giancana and According to James Files, Nicoletti was one of the gunmen who took part in the assassination of John F. Kennedy.

Charles Nicoletti was Sam Giancana's right hand from a young age. He was a violent Chicago Outfit gunman responsible for the death of his father and federal attempts on Fidel Castro's life, earning him a reputation as an effective contract killer. Nicoletti's driver said he had a special gun, a high-caliber Remington that fires one shot at a time. He was possibly involved in the assassination of the 35th US President, JFK. xx Episode 45: The Chicago Outfit- Charles Nicoletti: https://www.youtube.com/watch?v=q8K8mg25TB4

On March 29, 1977, in Chicago, Charles Nicoletti was shot dead three times in the back of the head. George De Mohrenschildt died the same day. Both men were due to appear before the Select House Committee on Assassinations about their involvement in the assassination of John F. Kennedy.

Eugene Hale Brading / Jim Braden

Eugene Hale Brading (also known as James Lee and Jim Braden) was arrested 35 times while living in California. He had convictions for burglary, illegal bookmaking, and embezzlement.

On November 21, 1963, Brading arrived in Dallas with Morgan Brown. They stayed at the Cabana Motel in suite 301. Later that day, Brading visited the offices of Texas oil billionaire Haroldson L. Hunt. Allegedly, Jack Ruby was also in the offices when Brading arrived.

After the assassination of John F. Kennedy, Brading was arrested and taken in for interrogation because he had been "acting suspiciously" in the Dal-Tex Building, overlooking Dealey Plaza. Brading told the police he was in Dallas on oil business and had gone into the building to make a phone call. Brading was released without charge and returned to his room at the Cabana Motel. Jack Ruby visited the motel around midnight.

Jack Lawrence

Jack Lawrence was a known marksman in the United States Air Force. He was a regular at the Carousel Club in Dallas, owned by Jack Ruby, and a close friend of George Senator, Ruby's roommate. Lawrence was a young man who worked as a salesman at a downtown Dallas Lincoln dealership. Lawrence claimed that Lee Harvey Oswald asked to test-drive a car in early November.

On November 21, 1963, Lawrence borrowed one of the showroom cars. The following day, he failed to turn up for work. According to Jim Marrs on *Crossfire,* about thirty minutes after the assassination, Lawrence came hustling through the company's showroom, pale and sweating with mud on his clothes. He rushed into the men's room and threw up. He told co-workers he had been ill that morning and that he had tried to drive the car back to the dealership but had to park it due to the heavy traffic.

Later, employees found the car parked behind the wooden picket fence on top of the Grassy Knoll overlooking Dealey Plaza. They reported the missing vehicle and Lawrence's strange behavior to the Dallas police, so Lawrence was interviewed by officers investigating the assassination. He left town after being released by police.

A lot of researchers say he may have been in the drain on Elm Street where JFK got hit and would have been able to get a shot at Kennedy as he came by. The drain tunnel came out into a creek, so he was muddy. I don't think he was one of the shooters, yet I think he was there. When you're in a manhole, all you can see is the street through a tight opening; with the car moving at that time, JFK wouldn't have been in his view.

Edward Lansdale

When President John F. Kennedy took office, Lansdale was appointed Assistant Secretary of Defense for Special Operations. He was trouble for the CIA. He argued the CIA should work closely with exiles in Cuba, particularly those with middle-class professions who opposed Fulgencio Batista and had become disillusioned with Fidel Castro because of his betrayal of the democratic process.

Lansdale was also opposed to the Bay of Pigs operation because he knew that it would not trigger a popular uprising against Castro. Kennedy respected Lansdale's advice and selected him to become the project leader of Operation Mongoose. Over 400 CIA officers were employed full-time on this project. But instead, Richard Bissell decided to arrange the assassination of Fidel Castro.

In September 1960, Bissell and Allen W. Dulles, the director of the CIA, initiated talks with two leading figures of the Mafia, Johnny Roselli and Sam Giancana. Later, other crime bosses, such as Carlos Marcello, Santos Trafficante, and Meyer Lansky, became involved in this plot against Castro.

Lansdale was involved in the assassination of the Diem brothers in Vietnam about three or four weeks before Kennedy. He did not take a shot, but he was there and, unfortunately, wasn't smart enough not to get his picture taken. There is a famous picture of these three drunk tramps. Lansdale was wearing a big ring, perhaps a West Point ring. Generals who saw the photo picked him out immediately and said that's Lansdale. So Lansdale was there and likely one of the people in charge of operations.

Charles Harrelson

Charles Harrelson was a civilian hitman who worked for the CIA and for anybody who would pay him. He is the father of actor Woody Harrelson.

Harrelson was born in Huntsville, Texas, in 1939. After leaving school, Harrelson moved to California, where he eventually became an encyclopedia salesman. He later turned to crime and, in 1960, was convicted of armed robbery. In their book *The Man on the Grassy Knoll*, John R. Craig and Philip A. Rogers claimed that Harrelson and Charles Rogers were the two gunmen behind the picket fence on the Grassy Knoll and were involved in the JFK assassination.

Harrelson, Rogers, and Chauncey Holt were the Three Tramps

arrested in Dealey Plaza on November 22, 1963.

In 1992 that the Dallas Police Department determined the Three Tramps were

Gus Abrams, John F. Gedney, and Harold Doyle.

CIA Set-Up to Conceal the Truth

In 1968, Harrelson was convicted for the murder of businessman Sam Degelia in a contract killing in South Texas and sentenced to 15 years in prison, but with time off for good behavior, he was free in five years.

In 1979, Harrelson was paid $250,000 by drug dealers to assassinate the federal judge John H. Wood. On May 29, 1979, Wood was shot dead as he left his Alamo Heights townhouse. Wood was known as "Maximum John" for his harsh sentences for drug traffickers. He was the first federal judge murdered in the 20th century.

When Harrelson was arrested, he confessed to being one of the gunmen who killed President Kennedy. He later withdrew that confession. Yet he was eventually convicted for the murder of Wood and received two life sentences.

In 1988, Harrelson told Nigel Turner, the producer of *The Men Who Killed Kennedy,* that "on November 22, 1963, at 12.30, I was at a restaurant in Houston, Texas, having lunch with a friend." He also told Turner that he would not have accepted such a contract to kill Kennedy. He knew if he had, he would have ended up, like Lee Harvey Oswald, being killed by the Mafia.

Loy Factor

Loy Factor was a well-known, fantastic shooter. He was a Chickasaw Indian, dirt poor, and brought in from Oklahoma. They paid him $10,000 to be on the sixth floor of the Texas School Book Depository building. I don't believe he took a shot, but he was there as another marksman.

Just before he died, he confessed to the JFK murder, telling Mark Collum and Glen Sample that he was one of three gunmen in the TSBD. Lee Harvey Oswald, Malcolm Wallace, and Ruth Paine were also there. Paine carried a walkie-talkie to communicate with the group. Paine was a friend of Marina Oswald, who was living with her at the time of the JFK assassination.

In *The Men on the Sixth Floor* (1995), the authors asked Loy, "What did they pay you $10,000 to do?" Loy stammered through an unconvincing explanation of how he merely assisted the group, that the woman was the radio operator, Oswald and the man who hired Loy were the shooters, and that he had been nothing more than some backup.

Roscoe White

Roscoe White joined the United States Marines and left for Japan in August 1957. He was stationed at Atsugi, worked on the U-2 project, and was a member of The Office of Naval Intelligence. White joined the Dallas Police Force in September 1963. Not long after, his wife, Geneva, claimed that she overheard her husband and Jack Ruby plotting the assassination of John F. Kennedy. He got on the Dallas police force three weeks before the assassination. So he wouldn't have time to even go through training.

White later told his wife he was in a trap. He was picked by Naval Intelligence to be a shooter because he was a good shot. But White didn't want to do it. Days before November 22, he kept saying, "I don't want to do it. I just don't want to do it. Either way, he's gonna kill me too." Who is "He?"

White eventually left the police force and was employed by a company called M & M Equipment as a welder. In September 1971, White and Richard Adair were both badly burnt in an industrial fire on the job. Adair recovered, but White died the following day. Some say it was a bomb planted by the CIA; it blew up, and White burned to death. The CIA got rid of all the people involved.

In September 1990, Roscoe's son, Ricky White, revealed during a meeting at the University of Texas that his father was involved in killing the President, JFK. Ricky said, "After my father shot the President, he handed his 7.65 Mauser to the man standing beside him. He grabbed the young military man's camera, hurled it over the fence, and ran through the parking lot, but his mother gave him that camera, so he screamed, "Just take the film. I want my camera back!""

White added that Lee Harvey Oswald had also taken part but had not fired any of the shots. Roscoe White, later that day, also killed J. D. Tippit, an 11-year veteran of the Dallas Police Department. Ricky White claimed he had gotten this information from his father's diary, which the FBI had taken away.

Roscoe's wife and son Ricky visited Roscoe's parents on a farm in Texas. Ricky's grandfather said, you know, your dad had some stuff in the garage. You might want to take a look at what's there. They find this chest, like one you take on a cruise ship, and open it up. It's filled with all kinds of stuff and a diary. Roscoe wrote how they made hiss father kill about 20 people.

Eugenio Martinez

Eugenio (Musculito) Martinez was born and raised in Cuba and moved to Miami after Fidel Castro gained power in 1959. Martinez became an active member of the anti-Castro Cuban Movement in the United States.

Some researchers believe Eugenio Martinez was involved in the assassination of John F. Kennedy. One source claims that Virgilio Gonzalez was the gunman in the Dal-Tex building, and Martinez was his spotter. On July 3, 1972, Martinez, Frank Sturgis, Virgilio Gonzalez, Bernard L. Barker, and James W. McCord were arrested while removing electronic devices from the Democratic Party campaign offices in an apartment block called Watergate—the phone number of CIA agent E. Howard Hunt was found in the address books of the burglars. Reporters were now able to link the break-in to the White House.

Bob Woodward, a reporter working for the *Washington Post*, was told by a friend employed by the government that senior aides of President Richard Nixon paid the burglars to obtain information about its political opponents.

In January 1973, Martinez, Frank Sturgis, E. Howard Hunt, Virgilio Gonzalez, Bernard L. Barker, Gordon Liddy, and James W. McCord were convicted of conspiracy, burglary, and wiretapping. Now released, Eugenio Martinez works in real estate in Miami, Florida.

Eddie Bayo

In the winter of 1962, Eddie Bayo of Alpha 66 claimed that two men in the Red Army, based at the Signals Intelligence facility near Havana, wanted to defect to the United States. They had details about atomic warheads and missiles that were still in Cuba, violating the publicly negotiated deal that the Soviets would dismantle the weapon sites in exchange for a pledge from the United States not to invade Cuba.

Several members of the anti-Castro community, including John Martino and Frank Sturgis, got involved with Bayo's story. William Pawley became convinced that helping get these Soviet officers out of Cuba was vitally important. David Sanchez Morales, another CIA agent we cover in this chapter, also became involved in this attempt to bring these two Soviet officers to the US.

However, in June 1963, their small group was unsuccessful in finding these Soviet officers in Cuba before their return to Miami. Bayo remained behind, and rumors circulated Bayo was captured and executed. However, his death went unreported in the Cuban press.

Orlando Bosch

Orlando Bosch was born on August 18, 1926 in Cuba. As a medical student at the University of Havana, he befriended Fidel Castro. Bosch put his liberal opinions into action and joined Fidel Castro in the campaign to remove Fulgencio Batista, the military dictator in Cuba.

Later, Bosch became disillusioned with the Movement and tried to organize a failed coup against Castro in 1960. Bosch and Luis

Posada Carriles, who both worked with the CIA at various times, were the founders of CORU, the Coordination of United Revolutionary Organizations, a militant group responsible for terrorist activities directed at the Cuban government of Fidel Castro. CORU activities included bombings and assassinations, including the killing of human-rights activist Orlando Letelier in Washington, DC, and the bombing of Cubana Flight 455, killing 73 people.

Bosch soon became disillusioned with the Castro government, and he left the country in July 1960. After the Bay of Pigs, Bosch ran an anti-Castro training camp for the Central Intelligence Agency in Homestead, Florida. Bosch gradually became convinced that President John F. Kennedy had betrayed the Cubans and wrote a pamphlet about this called The Tragedy of Cuba.

According to Marita Lorenz, Bosch became a member of Operation 40, a CIA assassination squad. A few days before the assassination of John F. Kennedy, a group including Bosch, Frank Sturgis, Guillermo Novo and Pedro Diaz Lanz, traveled to Dallas. Lorenz also claimed that Bosch was at a motel in Dallas to plan the Kennedy murder with the group.

Bosch founded the contra-revolutionary group called "Poder Cubano" (Cuban Power) as a means to develop and implement his terrorist theme of war throughout the world. According to Cuban authorities, Bosch was involved in 78 terrorist attacks on Spain, England, Japan, Mexico, Poland, and other countries that traded with Cuba.

In October 1968, United States officials arrested Bosch for terrorist activities. Ricardo Morales Navarrete provided evidence against Bosch, sentencing him to 10 years in prison, and released in 1972.

The following year, he moved to Venezuela and joined up with Guillermo Novo and Luis Posada. On November 25, 1975, leaders of the military intelligence services of Argentina, Bolivia, Chile, Paraguay, and Uruguay met with Juan Manuel Contreras in Santiago de Chile. The main objective was for the CIA to coordinate the actions of the various security services in "eliminating Marxist subversion."

Bosch soon became involved in this undercover operation, Operation Condor, given tacit approval by the United States, which feared a Marxist revolution in the region. The targets were officially leftist guerrillas and all kinds of political opponents.

In October 1976, a midair explosion of Cubana Flight 455 killed all 73 people aboard, including all 24 young athletes on Cuba's gold-medal fencing team. Police in Trinidad arrested two Venezuelans, Herman Ricardo and Freddy Lugo. Ricardo claimed Bosch and Luis Posada organized the bombing. Upon Posada's arrest, he was carrying a map of Washington showing the daily route of Orlando Letelier, the assassinated Chilean Foreign Minister, one month earlier, in September 1976. Herman Ricardo and Freddy Lugo were both sentenced to twenty years imprisonment.

In 1987 Bosch was freed with the help of Otto Juan Reich, the White House's leading adviser on Latin America. Bosch entered the United States, where he was granted asylum and eventually pardoned by President George Bush on July 18, 1990. Orlando Bosch died in Miami in April 2011.

Izquierdo

Nestor 'Tony' Izquierdo was born in the Matanzas Province in Cuba in 1936. He was a devoted Roman Catholic and worked with his father in a construction business. In 1959, Izquierdo joined anti-communist Manuel Artime's Rural Commandos and worked closely with the Catholic University Association (CUA) to plan a counter-revolution. Izquierdo left Cuba in 1960 and entered the United States via Mexico to establish the Movement for the Recovery of the Revolution (the MRR Party).

Izquierdo participated in the Bay of Pigs as a member of Brigade 2506. He worked closely with Rip Robertson and David Sanchez Morales in the many aggressive and successful raids against Cuba. Izquierdo worked under Frank Castro in the Halcones Dorados (Golden Hawks).

In 1963, Manuel Artime obtained funds from the CIA via Ted Shackley, head of the JM/WAVE station in Florida, to fund their initiatives. Nestor Izquierdo was involved in the assassination of John F. Kennedy. Independently of each other, James Richards and Gerry Hemming claim that Izquierdo was involved with the events in Dealey Plaza, specifically as a Dal-Tex spotter.

In April of 1977, Izquierdo was the subject of a U.S. Justice Department inquiry. His CIA case officer was Harold Feeney. Izquierdo, a devout anti-communist, fought the Sandinistas in Nicaragua. Nestor Izquierdo was killed in Nicaragua in a plane crash in 1979.

In honor of Izquierdo's constant fight against Communism and for his bravery, in 1992, Gilberto Casanova raised the necessary funds to construct a bronze statue of Nestor Izquierdo in Miami's Little Havana, created by sculptor Tony Lopez.

Mitchell WerBell

Mitchell WerBell, the son of a former Czarist cavalry officer, was born in Philadelphia in 1918. WerBell joined the Office of Strategic Services (OSS) during the Second World War and saw action in Burma and China. According to journalist Gaeton Fonzi, this enabled WerBell to join "the superspy fraternity" that included Allen W. Dulles, William Casey, Richard Helms, and E. Howard Hunt.

After the war, Werbell worked as an arms dealer and operated a series of weapon manufacturing firms, distributing advanced weaponry to selective foreign groups. In 1959, Werbell did covert work for Fulgencio Batista in Cuba. He became friends with Gerry P. Hemming and Bernardo De Torres, who worked as Werbell's representatives in his arms sales business.

Werbell was also rumored to be involved in the assassination of John F. Kennedy through Jack Ruby and supplied silencers used by the gunmen in Dallas. Author Gaeton Fonzi quoted Werbell as saying, "We don't play with people like that (Jack Ruby). I mean, it's as simple as that." Mitchell Livingston WerBell III died of cancer in 1983.

Virgillo (Villo) Gonzalez

Virgilio "Villo" R. González was a Cuban-born political activist, locksmith, and one of the five men arrested at the Democratic National Committee headquarters at the Watergate complex on June 17, 1972. The break-in led to the Watergate scandal and the eventual resignation of United States President Richard Nixon two years later.

After arriving in Miami, González became involved with the anti-Castro Movement and continued to work as a locksmith. CIA agent E recruited his lock-picking skills. Howard Hunt and Gonzalez's connection to Eugenio Martínez, to join the crew of Watergate burglars. The first break-in attempt was at midnight, but González did not have the right tools to get into the Democratic Party office. The second attempt was successful in picking the locks, and they were able to place bugs on three of the phones in the headquarters.

The group was required to break in again, take 1,440 photos of Democratic Party papers, and retrieve the bugs planted before. González had no problems with the lock this time, yet he noticed one of the three bug tapes they planted had gone missing. The group was discovered and arrested. Gonzalez pleaded guilty and spent 13 months in prison for the burglary.

When released from prison, González left the lock-picking business and ran a mechanic shop living in Miami with his second wife. He died in Miami on July 16, 2014, at age 88.

Loran Eugene Hall

Loran Eugene Hall was born in Newton, Kansas, in January 1930. He joined the US Army and later became a mercenary who joined the rebels led by Fidel Castro. Hall fell out with Castro, and in 1959, he spent several months in prison with cellmate Santo Trafficante.

On his release, Hall moved to the United States with Gerry P. Hemming, a member of the anti-Castro group Interpen (Intercontinental Penetration Force). Hall joined Hemming, Frank Sturgis, and David Ferrie in the International Anti-Communist Brigade.

In an interview he gave to the Select House Committee on Assassinations, Hall admitted he "was a radical right winger and a reactionary ... at almost every meeting that I ever went to, I heard somebody plotting to blow Kennedy's head off."

Hall participated in several raids on shipping around Cuba in February and March 1963 and was wounded in the leg. A few weeks later, Gerry P. Hemming introduced Hall to John Martino. Hall met Santo Trafficante, Sam Giancana, and Johnny Roselli at a Miami Beach hotel. Hall later reported that Giancana gave Eddie Bayo $15,000 as a down payment for a raid on Cuba. Bayo claimed that two officers in the Red Army wanted to defect to the United States.

Hall did not take part in the Bayo-Pawley raid as he became involved in a project to overthrow the government of Haiti. According to the author of *The Road to Dallas*, the invasion of Haiti involved John Martino, Irving Davidson, Roland Masferrer, and Carlos Marcello. The involvement suggests that while Masferrer reportedly hoped to establish an anti-Castro base in Haiti after overthrowing Duvalier, mob interests were looking forward to building some new casinos there."

Hall re-established contact with Santo Trafficante in Florida in 1963. In his book, *The Road to Dallas*, the historian David Kaiser claims Loran Hall had been involved in many discussions of assassination plots against Castro - including one failed attempt known as the Bayo-Pawley raid and had also heard a good deal of talk about assassinating President Kennedy.

In September 1963, a Cuban exile, Silvia Odio, received a visit from three men who claimed to be from New Orleans. Two of them were members of the Junta Revolucionaria. The third man, Leon, was introduced as an American sympathizer who was willing to take part in the assassination of Fidel Castro. After she told them that she was unwilling to get involved in any criminal activity, the three men left.

After the assassination of John F. Kennedy, Silvia Odio discovered that Leon was Lee Harvey Oswald. Odio gave evidence to the Warren Commission, and one of its lawyers commented: Silvia Odio was checked out thoroughly. The evidence is unanimously favorable that Odio is the most significant witness linking Oswald to the anti-Castro Cubans.

On September 16, 1964, FBI agent Leon Brown interviewed Loran Hall on behalf of the Warren Commission. Brown claims that Hall admitted that he visited a woman who could have been Silvia Odio. However, after Brown showed Hall a photograph of Odio, Hall claimed she was not the woman he met in New Orleans.

The FBI interviewed Silvia Odio again in October 1964. They showed her photographs of Loran Hall, William Seymour, Lawrence Howard, and Celio Castro Alga. She claimed none of the individuals were identical to the three men who had come to her apartment in Dallas in the last week of September 1963. Her sister, Annie Odio, was also in the apartment then and confirmed they were not the three individuals.

The author, Anthony Summers, suggests that the visit had been a deliberate ploy to link Junta Revolucionaria, a left-wing exile group, with the assassination. Hall later gave evidence before the Select House Committee on Assassinations and denied he told the FBI he visited Odio on September 25, 1963. Hall denied that he was involved in the assassination. However, in an interview he gave to *The Dallas Morning News,* he said right-wing activists working with CIA operatives wanted him to join the conspiracy to kill John F. Kennedy. According to Hall, he refused the contract. In another interview, Hall stated, "Hemming is a CIA punk, OK? I've known the SOB for fourteen years. He turned in his own goddam crews so he wouldn't have to go to Cuba. He's fingered me on my goddam deals and caused me to get arrested. Hey man, as it stands now, only two of us are left alive -- me and Santos Trafficante. And as far as I'm concerned, we're both going to stay alive - because I ain't gonna say shit."

However, during his testimony to the Select House Committee on Assassinations in May 1977, Hall makes it clear that he is referring to the Bayo-Pawley raid rather than the killing of Kennedy.

In September 1989, a federal drug conspiracy indictment in Tulsa named Loran Eugene Hall Sr., 59; his daughter, Barbara Ann Marteney, 34, of Mesquite; and his sons, Michael Stephen Hall, 36, of Burns, Kansas, and Loran Eugene Hall Jr., 34, of Derby, Kansas; and two other Kansas residents. The indictment charges that the elder Mr. Hall led the ring, which manufactured methamphetamine between October 1987 and February 1989. Loran Hall Jr. and Michael Hall pleaded guilty. Their father and sister remain at large."

During the trial of Loran Eugene Hall Jr., he claimed that a CIA operative set up a methamphetamine ring based in Mesquite to funnel money to the Contras in Nicaragua. Jim Heflet, a Tulsa attorney representing Hall, said his client believes the operation was a CIA front. "It may be true. There's quite an extensive history of his father's involvement," Heflet said. My client told me that a lot of his dad's involvement, specifically in the Kennedy assassination, has been sealed up, and we never may find out." Loran Hall died in Newton, Kansas, in April 1995. xx

https://spartacus-educational.com/JFKhallL.htm

Herminio Diaz Garcia

Herminio Diaz Garcia was born in Cuba in 1923. He was a cashier at the Hotel Habana-Rivera and a Cuban Restaurant Workers Union member. Later, he became involved in illegal activities and eventually became a bodyguard for Santos Trafficante.

Diaz Garcia killed Pipi Hernandez in 1948 at the Cuban Consulate in Mexico. In 1957, he was involved in an assassination attempt against President Jose Figures of Costa Rica. Diaz Garcia moved to the United States in July 1963, where he worked for Tony Varona. In December 1963, Dia Garcia was involved in an unsuccessful attempt to assassinate Fidel Castro. He was also involved in providing weapons to anti-Castro groups. Some researchers believe that Diaz Garcia was one of the gunmen who killed John F. Kennedy.

Diaz Garcia was killed on a mission at Monte Barreto in the Miramar district of Cuba in May 1966 and is buried in Columbus, Havana. xx https://spartacus-educational.com/JFKgarciaH.htm

Charles Rogers

Charles Rogers, born in 1921, studied nuclear physics at the University of Houston. During the Second World War, he served with the Organization of Naval Intelligence. After the war, Rogers worked as a seismologist with Shell Oil. While a member of the Civil Air Patrol, he became a close friend of David Ferrie's and joined the CIA in 1956.

Rogers was accused of being involved in the assassination of John F. Kennedy. Gibson claimed that Rogers was "Frenchy," one of the three tramps, along with W and Chauncey Holt, arrested in Dealey

Plaza on November 22, 1963. After his release, Rogers left the country on a CIA plane to South America. 2) Blowup from a tramp photo showing "Frenchy." This was Harold Doyle--whom the man much more resembles than he does Charles Rogers.

In the 1992 book *The Man on the Grassy Knoll*, John R. Craig and Philip A. Rogers claimed that Rogers was the Lee Harvey Oswald imposter who traveled to Mexico City the month before the assassination. The authors argue that Rogers and Charles Harrelson were the two gunmen behind the picket fence on the Grassy Knoll.

On June 23, 1965, Charles Rogers's parents, Fred and Edwina Rogers, were found murdered in Houston, Texas. Officer Charles Bullock later reported," "I opened the refrigerator and saw nothing but meat stacked in it. My partner standing next to me made the comment that it looked like somebody had butchered a hog. We didn't know it was a body until we got ready to close the refrigerator, and we could see the (human) head down in the bottom of the vegetable bin."

Charles Rogers was the chief suspect, but he disappeared and has not been seen since. The private detective, John R. Craig, claims that Rogers continued to work for the CIA in South America and was part of the Iran-Contra program. Another report says he was murdered in Honduras.

In October 1991, Chauncey Holt confessed to John Craig, Phillip Rogers, and Gary Shaw about his role in the assassination of John F. Kennedy. Holt's story was sabotaged in 1992 when the Dallas Police Department revealed that the three tramps were Gus Abrams, John F. Gedney, and Harold Doyle.

Ray and Mary LaFontaine carried out their personal research into this claim. They traced Doyle and Gedley, who confirmed they were two of the tramps in the photograph. Gus Abrams was dead, but his sister identified him as the third tramp in the picture.

Chapter 10

20 People Who Knew About the JFK Murder Before it Happened

If You Knew in Advance, What Would You Do?

Number 1

Richard Case Nagell

Richard Case Nagell was born in Greenwich, New York, on August 5, 1930. Educated in Albany, Nagell joined the United States Army in 1948. During the Korean War, he was awarded the Bronze Star and the Purple Heart and, at the age of twenty, became one of the youngest men in history to receive a field promotion to the rank of Captain.

In November 1954, Nagell suffered severe injuries in an air crash. According to Nagell, when he recovered, he began working for the CIA as a double agent. This involved becoming an activist in the American Communist Party. This included distributing Marxist propaganda in Mexico.

Nagell also claimed he was involved in monitoring a group of Cuban exiles plotting against Fidel Castro. In 1963, Nagell discovered that this group was planning to assassinate John F. Kennedy while making it appear that it had been ordered by Castro. When he told the KGB, they ordered him to warn Lee Harvey Oswald about what was happening. Nagell also claimed he warned the FBI and CIA about the plot.

In September 1963, Nagell walked into a bank in El Paso, Texas, fired two shots into the ceiling, and then waited to be arrested. Nagell claimed he did this to isolate himself from the assassination plot. This was successful, and Nagell was charged with armed robbery and ended up spending the next five years in prison.

On his release, Nagell told Jim Garrison about his knowledge of the assassination of John F. Kennedy. He claimed that David Ferrie, Guy Banister, and Clay Shaw were involved in this plot with Lee Harvey Oswald. However, Garrison decided against using him as a witness in the court case against Shaw.

Dick Russell wrote about Nagell in his book, *The Man Who Knew Too Much* (1992). Nagell claimed the initial plan to assassinate President John F. Kennedy was financed by Haroldson L. Hunt and other individuals. The operation was to be performed by an anti-Castro group. According to Nagell, the conspirators believed that if they set up Lee Harvey Oswald, a well-known supporter of Fidel Castro with links to the Soviet Union, the assassination would result in a full-scale war against Cuba.

Richard Case Nagell was found dead on November 1, 1995. A spokesman for the Los Angeles Coroner's Office said Nagell had a history of heart disease and that his body was discovered on the floor of the bathroom at his home in Rampart, Los Angeles. Richard Case

Nagel somehow got involved in planning the Kennedy assassination. Once they blamed it on Oswald, his job was to kill Oswald. But he didn't want to do that. It's unknown why, and most of the investigators believed that he did not want to be associated with the actual assassination of the American president.

To protect himself from getting killed by the Assassination Planners, he pulled the bank stunt in El Paso to land himself in jail on purpose. He thought he would get six months or maybe a year in jail because he didn't actually rob anything. But he was incarcerated for five years. He was one of the last people to die who knew pretty much everything about the assassination and was thought to be the last man alive who could straighten out the whole conspiracy for history.

Number 2

Joseph Milteer

Joseph Milteer, from Georgia, was active in the Klu Klux Klan and other right-wing organizations, like the Minutemen. He visited a friend who lived in Florida, #20 on our list, Willie Somersett, who happened to be a confidential informant for a detective in Miami.

They were talking in general, and then it got around to the Kennedy situation, so Somersett recorded the conversation. The recording is available online, on YouTube, and cited here from Anthony Summers' book *Conspiracy* and recounts the following edited version of Milteer's conversation with Somersett:

INFORMANT: I think Kennedy is coming here on the 18th, or something like that, to make some kind of speech . . .

EXTREMIST: You can bet your bottom dollar he is going to have a lot to say about the Cubans. There are so many of them here.

INFORMANT: Yeah. Well, he will have a thousand bodyguards; don't worry about that.

EXTREMIST: The more bodyguards he has, the easier it is to get him.

INFORMANT: Well, how in the hell do you figure would be the best way to get him?

EXTREMIST: From an office building with a high-powered rifle. . . He knows he's a marked man . . . .

INFORMANT: They are really going to try to kill him?

EXTREMIST: Oh yeah, it is in the working . . . .

INFORMANT: Boy, if that Kennedy gets shot, we have to know where we are at. Because you know that will be a real shake if they do that.

EXTREMIST: They wouldn't leave any stone unturned there, no way. They will pick somebody up within hours afterward if anything like that happens. Just to throw the public off.

Then, in a long footnote (p. 624), Summers adds the following:

Joseph Milteer, the right-wing extremist who said two weeks before the assassination that the President's murder was "in the working," told a police informant afterward that "Everything ran true to form. I guess you thought I was kidding you when I said he would be killed from a window with a high-powered rifle." Asked whether he was guessing when he made the original remark, Milteer replied, "I don't do any guessing." According to the informant, Milteer said there was no need "to worry about Lee Harvey Oswald getting caught because he doesn't know anything." The right-wing, said Milteer, was "in the clear," adding that "the patriots have outsmarted the Communist group in order that the Communists would carry out the plan without the right-wing becoming involved."

Again, note that Milteer takes "credit" for knowing that Kennedy was going to be "killed from a window with a high-powered rifle." This is the Warren Commission's version of what happened. More to the point, it was the version that law enforcement officials and the media were publicizing when Milteer talked to Somersett.

Rather than having "inside knowledge" that the media were pushing an inaccurate account, Milteer *accepts* what law enforcement officials and the media were saying! He does seem to accept that Oswald is a "patsy" that has been manipulated. But he says a "communist group" was manipulated by "the patriots" (presumably, Milteer's racist buddies) to do the killing.

A more complete account of what Milteer told Somersett is found in an article in the September 1976 issue of *Miami Magazine* by Dan Christensen. Titled "JFK, King: The Dade County Links," it provides details omitted from conspiracy books.

Somerset: ...I think Kennedy is coming here on the 18th...to make some kind of speech...I imagine it will be on TV.

Milteer: You can bet your bottom dollar he is going to have a lot to say about the Cubans.   There are so many of them here.

Somersett: Yeah, well, he will have a thousand bodyguards. Don't worry about that.

Milteer: The more bodyguards he has the easier it is to get him.

Somersett: Well, how in the hell do you figure would be the best way to get him?

Milteer: From an office building with a high-powered rifle. How many people does he have going around who look just like him? Do you now about that?

Somersett: No, I never heard he had anybody.

Milteer: He has about fifteen. Whenever he goes anyplace, he knows he is a marked man.

Somersett: You think he knows he is a marked man?

Milteer: Sure he does.

Somersett: They are really going to try to kill him?

Milteer: Oh yeah, it is in the working. Brown himself, [Jack] Brown, is just as likely to get him as anybody in the world. He hasn't said so, but he tried to get Martin Luther King.

After a few more minutes of conversation, Somersett again spoke of assassination.

Somersett: Hitting this Kennedy is going to be a hard proposition, I tell you. I believe you may have figured out a way to get him, the office building, and all that. I don't know how the Secret Service agents cover all them office buildings everywhere he is going. Do you know whether they do that or not?

Milteer: Well, if they have any suspicion, they do that, of course. But without suspicion,   chances are that they wouldn't. You take there in Washington. This is the wrong time of the year, but in pleasant weather, he comes out of the veranda and somebody could be in a hotel room across the way and pick him off just like that.

Somersett: Is that right?

Milteer: Sure, disassemble a gun. You don't have to take a gun up there; you can take it up in pieces. All those guns come knock down. You can take them apart. Before the end of the tape, the conversation returns to Kennedy.

Milteer: Well, we are going to have to get nasty...

Somersett: Yeah, get nasty.

Milteer: We have got to be ready; we have got to be sitting on go, too.

Somersett: Yeah, that is right.

Milteer: There ain't any count-down to it; we have just go to be sitting on go. Countdown,   they can move in on you, and on go, they can't.

The countdown is all right for a slow, prepared operation. But in an emergency operation, you have got to be sitting on the go.

Somersett: Boy, if that Kennedy gets shot, we have got to know where we are at. Because you know that will be a real shake...

Milteer: They wouldn't leave any stone unturned there. No way. They will pick somebody within hours afterward if anything like that would happen, just to throw the public off.

Somersett: Oh, somebody is going to have to go to jail if he gets killed.

Milteer: Just like Bruno Hauptmann in the Lindbergh case, you know.

It seems the conspiracy books leave some things out. They usually don't tell readers about:

1. The 15 look-alikes that Kennedy has traveling with him? If you're going to shoot Kennedy, you wouldn't want to hit one a' them look-alikes, would you?

2. The fact that Milteer named the man who was supposedly going to kill Kennedy — one Jack Brown — and nobody has linked him to the assassination. Interestingly, after the assassination, Brown was forgotten.

3. The fact that the language about taking a disassembled gun up into a tall building was in the context of shooting Kennedy on the veranda of the White House in warm weather.

It seems that presenting Milteer as "The Miami Prophet" (Marrs' term for him) rather than "The Quitman Crackpot" requires withholding information from your readers.

Number 3

Rose Cheramie

Rose Cheramie (Cherami) was found unconscious by the side of the road at Eunice, Louisiana, on 20th November 1963. Lieutenant Francis Frugé of the Louisiana State Police took her to the state hospital. **Used by Jack Ruby as a mule.** On the journey, Cheramie said that she had been thrown out of a car by two gangsters who worked for Jack Ruby. She claimed that the men were involved in a plot to kill John F. Kennedy.

Cheramie added that Kennedy would be killed in Dallas within a few days. Later she told the same story to doctors and nurses who treated her. As she appeared to be under the influence of drugs, her story was ignored. Following the assassination, Cheramie was interviewed by the police. She claimed that Lee Harvey Oswald had visited Ruby's nightclub. She believed the two men were having a homosexual relationship. Upon arrival in Houston, she repeated this claim to Captain Morgan but refused to talk to federal authorities, saying she didn't want to get involved in this mess. According to Lt. Fruge, the information Rose Cherami supplied about the narcotics ring was "true and good information."

Rose Cheramie was found dead on 4th September 1965. At first, it appeared she had been involved in a road accident. Later, it was argued that she had been shot in the head before being run over by a car to disguise the original wound. However, the Louisiana State Police Memo reported: "Cheramie died of injuries received from an automobile accident on a strip of highway near Big Sandy, Texas, in the early morning of September 4, 1965. The driver stated Cheramie had been lying in the roadway, and although he attempted to avoid hitting her, he ran over the top of her skull, causing fatal injuries. An investigation into the accident and the possibility of a relationship between the victim and the driver produced no evidence of foul play. The case was closed." The Texas authorities were uninterested.

Number 4

Robert Tosh Plumlee

Tosh Plumlee was born in 1937. He joined the United States Army in April 1954 and was assigned to the Texas 49th Armored Division. Later, he was transferred to Dallas, where he joined the 4th Army Reserve Military Intelligence Unit.

After leaving the Army, Plumlee worked as an aircraft mechanic before obtaining his pilot's license in 1956.

Soon afterwards he began work as a pilot for clandestine CIA flights. This included working for William Harvey, Tracy Barnes, and Rip Robertson. Plumlee also transported arms to Cuba before Castro took power. Plumlee was also associated with Operation 40.

In 1962, Plumlee was assigned to Task Force W which operated at the time from the JM/WAVE station in Miami. Plumlee claimed that in November 1963, he was a co-pilot on a top-secret flight supported by the CIA. Plumlee's flight left Florida on 21st November and stopped in New Orleans and Houston before reaching Dallas in the early morning hours of 22nd November. On board was Johnny Roselli. Plumlee testified that their assignment was to stop the planned assassination of John F. Kennedy.

Tosh Plumlee testified in 2004: "When I later learned Oswald had been arrested as the lone assassin, I remembered having met him on a number of previous occasions which were connected with the intelligence training matters first at Illusionary warfare training in Nags Head, North Carolina." Dr. Proctor: So here we had some young man, Lee Oswald, who, as far as we know, was a very happy Marine, given the opportunity to serve his country in a clandestine way. He wasn't picked up by Soviet intelligence, so he came back. He's going around trying to find out who he is and what he can do *and gets caught up in something that he has no idea what the outcome is going to be.*

Plumlee worked as an undercover operative and contract pilot for the federal government during the "Drug War" during the presidency of Ronald Reagan. In 1977, Plumlee testified before Frank Church and his Select Committee on Intelligence Activities. He also testified before the Senate Foreign Relations Committee in 1990 and 1991.

Number 5

John Roselli

John Roselli (Filippo Sacco) first became involved in crime when he worked for Al Capone in the 1920s. By the end of the Second World War, Roselli had emerged as a senior crime boss in Las Vegas with close links to Meyer Lansky.

Roselli is like a storybook character. In the movies he would be cast as a gangster. He was a handsome guy and very outgoing; he was known as the Godfather of the West Coast. So whenever they decided to kill Castro, the United States and the Kennedys were in agreement with Kellyanne Castro.

In March 1960, President Dwight Eisenhower of the United States approved a Central Intelligence Agency (CIA) plan to overthrow Fidel Castro. The plan involved a budget of $13 million to train "a paramilitary force outside Cuba for guerrilla action." The strategy was organized by Richard Bissell and Richard Helms. Richard Bissell was the second highest man in the CIA at that time under Allen Dulles, who was responsible for major projects such as the U-2 spy plane and the Bay of Pigs Invasion. He is seen as one of the most important spymasters in CIA history.

Sidney Gottlieb of the CIA Technical Services Division was asked to come up with proposals that would undermine Castro's popularity with the Cuban people. Plans included a scheme to spray a television studio in which he was about to appear with a hallucinogenic drug and contaminate his shoes with thallium, which they believed would cause the hair in his beard to fall out.

These schemes were rejected, and instead, Bissell decided to arrange the assassination of Fidel Castro. In September 1960, Richard Bissell and Allen W. Dulles, the director of the Central Intelligence Agency (CIA), initiated talks with two leading figures of the Mafia, Roselli (using the name John Rawlston) and Sam Giancana.

On 12th March 1961, William Harvey arranged for CIA operative Jim O'Connell to meet Sam Giancana, Santo Trafficante, Johnny Roselli, and Robert Maheu at the Fontainebleau Hotel. During the meeting, O'Connell gave poison pills and $10,000 to Rosselli to be used against Fidel Castro. As Richard D. Mahoney points out in his book *Sons and Brothers, The days of Jack and Bobby Kennedy* (1999): "Late one evening, probably March 13, Rosselli passed the poison pills and the money to a small, reddish-haired Afro-Cuban by the name of Rafael "Macho" Gener in the Boom Boom Room, a location Giancana thought stupid.

Rosselli's purpose, however, was not just to assassinate Castro but to set up the Mafia's partner in crime, the United States government. Accordingly, he was laying a long, bright trail of evidence that unmistakably implicated the CIA in the Castro plot. This evidence, whose purpose was blackmail, would prove critical in the CIA's cover-up of the Kennedy assassination.

Johnny Roselli was on the plane that Tosh Plumlee flew to Dallas on the morning of the assassination. Supposedly, it was told by Roselli that it was an aborted attempt. There were two other men on the plane with Roselli, yet Tosh doesn't know who they were. They might have been Cubans, or they might have been Corsicans.

Rosselli was to be one of the first people to be interviewed by the HSCA but went missing in July 1976. His body was later discovered in the Intracoastal Waterway in North Miami. He had been cut up and stuffed into a 55-gallon steel drum.

Number 6

Albert Osbourne

Shocking confession of British-born 'Soviet spy' to his family in Grimsby is revealed in astonishing letter:

Albert Osborne wrote a letter to the family months after John F Kennedy was killed.

Osborne, of Grimsby, told his parents that he was being hunted by the FBI.

Osborne reveals that he was accused of befriending assassin Lee Harvey Oswald. He said in the letter that they traveled on a bus together from Mexico to Texas. Osborne is also believed to have tipped off the British press that JFK would be killed. The call to Cambridge Press came 25 minutes before Kennedy was assassinated.

LONDON — Twenty-five minutes before John F. Kennedy was assassinated, a British newspaper received an anonymous tip about "some big news" in the United States, according to the trove of more than 2,800 documents released late Thursday by the National Archives.

The mystery call was made to a senior reporter at the *Cambridge News*, a paper that serves the East Anglia area of eastern England, on Nov. 22, 1963, at 6:05 p.m. local time. Kennedy was shot shortly afterward as he rode in a presidential motorcade in Dallas, Texas, at 12:30 p.m. CST. Dallas is six hours behind Britain.

"The caller said only that the Cambridge News reporter should call the American Embassy in London for some big news and then hung up," the memo from the CIA's James Angleton to FBI director J. Edgar Hoover said.

The revelation, one of many that emerged from the planned release of the Kennedy assassination documents — so far, there are no smoking guns — adds to the raft of conspiracy theories surrounding his death. In fact, the memo was first released in July but went unreported until the cache of files was released Thursday.

The memo, dated Nov. 26, 1963, says: "After the word of the President's death was received, the reporter informed the Cambridge police of the anonymous call, and the police informed MI5. The important point is that the call was made, according to MI5 calculations, about 25 minutes before the President was shot. The Cambridge reporter had never received a call of this kind before, and MI5 stated that he is known to them as a sound and loyal person with no security record."

MI5 is Britain's domestic security agency. The reporter's name was not mentioned in the memo, which adds that MI5 had received "similar anonymous phone calls of a strangely coincidental nature."

The *Cambridge News* noted in a story Friday that it, too, did not know the name of the reporter who took the call, although it said the existence of the memo was first discovered by a lawyer, Michael

116

Eddowes, who devoted much of his life to investigating the mystery surrounding Kennedy's death

Eddowes, who died in 1992, told the *Cambridge News* in 1981 that he believed the anonymous caller was a British-born Soviet agent named Albert Osborne.

Two months before Kennedy's assassination, Eddowes believed that Osborne, who also apparently used the alias John Howard Bowen, had befriended Lee Harvey Oswald, the man ultimately charged with murdering Kennedy.

Eddowes' theory was that the call was made "because the Soviet Union was eager that the assassination should be seen as a conspiracy," according to the paper. It was not clear why the *Cambridge News* was specifically chosen or why the call was made to a local paper as opposed to a national one, which may have led to greater exposure.

Number 7

David Christensen

Flight Sergeant David F. Christensen claimed that in the run-up to Kennedy's death, he had intercepted an encrypted communication between certain individuals in the Cuban Government and an individual well-known in the organized crime world, plotting the assassination. His attempts to get the intercept to the

NSA were thwarted, causing him (he claimed) to have a mental breakdown, a divorce, etc etc.

Conversely, others say that this never happened, that searches of the files revealed nothing ("*recognizing that most records from this period no longer exist*"), that Christensen suffered from alcoholism and family problems, etc etc.

I can't judge either way, but I thought it would be good (a) to include links to the various NSA scans and (b) to properly transcribe the letter Christensen wrote, which is what I did here.

The letter from Christensen to his former colleague Sgt Michael B. Stevensen at "Corry" Field, Florida, is included here:

David F. Christensen

V.A. Hospital

Sheridan, WY 82801

Nick,

Well, after 13 1/ 2 years, I finally found out your whereabouts. Dam, its been a long time since Kirknewton, Scotland, and the beer we drank on the beach and the club. Had to get your address from the outfit in Texas.

Nick, whatever happened to Sgt Prater. If you know his whereabouts, please send me his address. How in the hell have you been doing?

Nick, I had a nervous breakdown. Plus, in 74, my leg shattered in over a hundred places. Things have really gone to hell for me. I'm working with the vet benefits counselor, who is an ex 203. Speaking of 203's, where the hell is Frenchy? You know the little guy. What

I'm going to say is no longer classified, so don't get all shit shook. I've done checked it out.

Christ, you remember the position I worked at, in Sgt Praters section, don't you? You remember about a month or 6 weeks before I left Scotland when I picked up a link mentioning the assassination of President Kennedy. How hard I tried to get it sent out, and because of that fuckin Forney and Delaughter, they wouldn't send it to NSA. Since I have learned that the man's name; most mentioned, was number 4 in a certain branch of organized crime at the time. Was number 2 last year. I will send you a form for proof of claim.

This guy here, "the 203," says I should be getting a service-connected disability for my nerves. The "link was" Lisbon to Tangiers , you remember. How I got my ass chewed for not dropping the link. Have learned that this branch of crime often will put out a feeler of forthcoming things. By sending it as a practice message.

Nick, it really broke me up after Nov. 22, 63. Especially when I had it all beforehand. It was first like the 202's said, Ha. I was nuts when the Russians first came out with the ITI & B's. Later proved them wrong, didn't I. That was another first for us, as I recall. Duane Bruntz from Baker Trick put up a good support of my claim. I'm sending you this certified so to make sure you get it. As I recall you should be able to B.S. them good enough to help me.

I know it cost me a divorce and everything from my wife. Christ, you remember Marlene, don't you? That good-looking little 1/2 Indian girl from N. Dak. Nick, when you get this form, send it back to me, and I'll let the vets benefit guy to send it in. Being a M.Sgt, I think you know how to bull shit pretty good. Also, do you know Sgt Harley and Sgt Willy Hendrickson's address? I guess old Garnett K.

Tatum retired. Wonder what ghetto, he is living in, Ha! What in the hell are you doing in Florida, anyhow? Be sure to put emphasis on my nerves going to hell and not giving a shit about my work after the interception of the message.

Y Y Prosign

Your old buddy from the Berkely Bar

Here is a link to an online memorial to David Frederick Christensen :

David passed away Monday, December 22, 2008, at his home in Killdeer, ND. David Frederick Christensen was born January 26, 1942, to Ole and Hazel (Lodnell) Christensen in Dickinson, ND. He grew up on a ranch near Halliday and attended schools, graduating from Halliday High School in 1960. David and Marlene Burr were married in 1960, and to this union, two sons were born, Michael and David. David enlisted in the US Air Force and served with the Radio Intelligence in the Scotland Unit. He was honorably discharged in 1963. He then returned to the home ranch in the Halliday area. David began working in the oilfields, which took him to various places in the western United States. He enjoyed rodeos, playing pinochle and time spent with his family. David is survived by his two sons, Michael (Bobbie) Christensen, Rapid City, SD, and David (Georgette) Christensen, Apple Valley, MN; a first cousin, Patricia (Pat)(Phil) Braeger, Watertown, SD; six grandchildren, Haley Christensen, Tyler Christensen, Jordan Christensen, Justin Christensen, Benjamin

Christensen, and Kendra Christensen. He is preceded in death by both parents.

Number 8 & 9 Irv and Karyn Kupcinet

Irving Kupcinet, the son of a truck driver, was born in North Lawndale on 31st July 1912. After graduating from the University of North Dakota, he joined the Philadelphia Eagles of the National Football League. A serious shoulder injury resulted in him giving up football, and in 1935 became a sports writer with the *Chicago Sun-Times*.

In 1948, Kupcinet was given his own column for the *Chicago Sun-Times*. Over the years, his column was distributed to more than 100 newspapers around the world.

In 1952, Kupcinet became a television talk show host on CBS. Five years later, he replaced Jack Parr on NBC's America After the Dark, which eventually became The Tonight Show. He also appeared in two movies produced by Otto Preminger, Anatomy of a Murder (1959) and Advise and Consent (1962). His daughter, Karyn Kupcinet, became an actress and appeared in The Ladies' Man (1961).

Irv Kupcinet knew Jack Ruby in Chicago in the 1940s. According to W. Penn Jones, Irv kept in contact with Ruby and discovered that he was involved in a plot to assassinate President John F. Kennedy. Jones argues that Irv passed this information on to his daughter, Karyn. In his book *Forgive My Grief*, Jones reports that "a few days before the assassination, Karyn Kupcinet, 23, was trying to place a long-distance telephone call from the Los Angeles area. According to reports, the long-distance operator heard Miss Kupcinet scream into the telephone that President Kennedy was going to be killed.

Karyn Kupcinet's body was discovered on 30th November 1963. Police estimated that she had been dead for two days. The New York Times reported that she had been strangled. Her actor boyfriend, Andrew Prine, was the main suspect, but he was never charged with the murder, and the crime remains unsolved.

Some researchers claimed that there was a link between the death of Kupcinet and the assassination of John F. Kennedy. It was argued that the conspirators were trying to frighten off Kupcinet from telling what he knew. Kupcinet rejected this idea. He wrote in the *Chicago Sun-Times* (9th November 1992): "The NBC *Today Show* on Friday carried a list of people who died violently in 1963 shortly after the death of President John F. Kennedy and may have had some link to the assassination. The first name on the list was Karyn Kupcinet, my daughter. That is an atrocious outrage. She did die violently in a Hollywood murder case still unsolved. That same list was published in a book years ago with no justification or verification. The book left the impression that some on the list may have been killed to silence them because of their knowledge of the assassination. Nothing could be further from the truth in my daughter's case."

Irv Kupcinet died of pneumonia in Chicago, Illinois, on 11th November 2003.

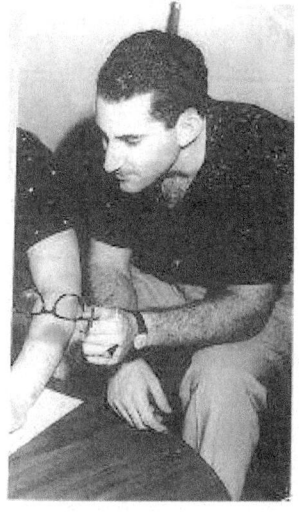

Number 10

Eugene Dinkin

Private First Class Eugene Dinkin was a cryptographic code operator stationed in Metz, France. On November 4, 1963, he went AWOL from his unit and entered Switzerland using forged travel orders and a false Army identification card. On November 6, he appeared in the Press Room of the United Nations in Geneva and told reporters he was being persecuted. He also told reporters that "they" were plotting against President Kennedy and that "something" would happen in Dallas.

After Kennedy was murdered, a friend of Dinkin's named Dennis De Witt told military authorities that Dinkin had predicted Kennedy's assassination for November 28 and later changed the date to November 22.

Dinkin was arrested on November 13 and placed in a psychiatric hospital, and later transferred to Walter Reed, where he underwent various psychological tests before eventually being released. His allegation reached the White House on November 29 and went to the Warren Commission in April of 1964.

Retellings of the Dinkin story typically note his status as a crypto operator and speculate that he may have learned of an assassination plot decrypting military communications, perhaps between military plotters and Marseilles assassins. But the FBI reports on Dinkin, including interviews with him conducted in April 1964, state that the allegations came about from Dinkin's study of military publications such as *Stars and Stripes*. Dinkin told the FBI that it was his study of "psychological sets" that revealed to him both an anti-Kennedy bias as well as a military plot in the works. How we could divine the latter, and in particular attach dates and places for the upcoming murder, is hard to imagine.

One explanation would be that Dinkin indeed learned about a plot through his crypto assignment and that something about his confinement at Walter Reed led him to suppress this in favor of the story the FBI reported. An opposing view would, of course, be that he was a paranoid individual who happened to make a lucky guess.

One method of determining the truth would have been to interview his military associates to see what he told them about where his ideas came from, including those named by Dinkinin in his FBI interviews: PFC Dennis De Witt, PFC Larry Pulles, Sgt. Walter Reynolds, and R. Thomas. The FBI, after taking these names, does not appear to have followed up on them. The Warren Commission took no interest in the matter and indeed omitted any mention of Dinkin from its purportedly encyclopedic 26 volumes of evidence.

Number 11

Abraham Bolden

Abraham Bolden joined the Chicago Secret Service in 1960. His fateful encounter with JFK was at the Chicago convention center in April 1961, where the president arrived for a political event. JFK stopped at the bathroom door and asked Bolden, "Has there ever been a Negro Secret Service agent on White House detail in Washington DC?" When Bolden replied no, Kennedy asked him if he would like to be the first. Bolden was 26 years old.

At the White House, Bolden began to notice breathtaking lapses in security that foreshadowed how Kennedy was left as a sitting duck, his Secret Service practically non-existent. Bolden was harassed by his fellow agents because he accused them of missing shifts, drinking heavily on the job, and using their vehicles to transport women and visit bars. Bolden took his concerns to the Secret Service Director, James Rowley, but were ignored.

One day in his office, Bolden reclined in his chair to answer a call, and looking up, he saw a noose hanging from the ceiling above him.

Bolden believes this led to his demotion back to the Chicago field office after only a few months on the White House detail.

In October 1963, while Bolden was working on counterfeit cases in the Chicago office, a message came from the FBI headquarters that the assassination plot against JFK involving a squad of Cuban exiles had just been uncovered. Two of the suspects were renting a motel room along the route of an upcoming presidential motorcade in Chicago. Their plan was foiled when a maid told the motel's manager she discovered several high-powered rifles and maps of the president's November 2 parade route in one of the rooms. The Secret Service arrested the Cubans, who then, astonishingly, were released shortly thereafter, prior to JFK's scheduled arrival.

According to Bolden, JFK canceled his trip on the morning of November 2 upon receiving a phone call from the agent in charge of the Chicago Secret Service office, warning of the threat -- not only from the at-large Cubans but also, tantalizingly, from a mysterious ex-Marine with remarkable similarities to Lee Harvey Oswald, soon to be the accused assassin of President Kennedy in Dallas. He was released, too, yet marked as a *perfect patsy* for the assassination plan.

After JFK's murder, Bolden was tenacious in getting the Chicago incident evidence to the Warren Commission. He was dumbfounded to learn this information about an assassination conspiracy -- three weeks before November 22, 1963 -- was not being investigated by the Warren Commission.

In May 1964, Bolden was sent to Washington for retraining, and the day he arrived he was pulled out of class and flown back to Chicago due to an emergency back in Chicago. He was driven to the US attorney's office in Chicago and taken into custody. He was framed for taking a $50,000 bribe for a government file and sentenced to six years in prison, almost killed while there, and released after three years. It is common knowledge today that it was a setup.

On April 26, 2022, President Joe Biden pardoned Abraham Bolden, at 87-years-old, who was the first Black man to join the Secret Service Security detail.

Number 12

Elizabeth Cole (A set-up)

Elizabeth Cole was a student at Hunter College in New York City. While attending a Foreign Students Convention at Rutgers University in New Jersey, she met a young Cuban man from Fairleigh Dickinson University who said he had friends involved in the Bay of Pigs invasion. Cole described the Cuban as being very angry at the situation. While attempting to use a pay phone to call her parents, Cole, who was bilingual, saw the phone was in use by the Cuban student. Speaking to someone in Spanish. He spoke of a plot to assassinate President John F. Kennedy. Details like the book company and the city of Dallas to be the location where the assassination was to take place. She also heard the student mention that an unnamed high-ranking government official would afford aid and/or protection to the people involved.

HSCA Administrative Folder N6, JFK Miscellaneous Information, Volume 1. Subject was interviewed at her home in Wayne NJ.

Number 13

Jorge Martinez Soto (A set-up)

Warren Commission document #26 FBI File $105-82555 Field Office File #105-8342

In November 1963, Lillian Springler worked in the gift shop at the Parrot Jungle in Miami, Florida. A Cuban man browsing the shop struck up a conversation with Lillian about politics, and aggressively, he started speaking of shooting President Kennedy *between the eyes*. The unknown man added that his friend Lee served in the military, was a sharpshooter, and lived in either Texas or Mexico. He spoke several languages fluently, including Russian.

After the JFK assassination, the Parrot Jungle mystery man was identified as Jorge Martinez. He admitted to speaking to Ms. Springler, yet said she must have misunderstood him.

Now, it would seem odd when you think about the fearlessness of what Ms. Springer did. However, any concerned person would tell friends and call the police to report that this erratic man came into the shop talking about killing Kennedy. Martinez looked like Lee Harvey Oswald, so was he a put-up job, too? Several *put-up jobs* like this were organized so the Kennedy conspirators would have witnesses for the trial.

Number 14

Adele Edisen: A set-up (plant)

On 22 April 1963, a neuroscientist named Adele Edison was having dinner at *Blackie's House of Beef* in Washington with another doctor, Jose Rivera, whom she met earlier that month at a biomedical convention in New Jersey.

Among the various topics they discussed, two stood out: Rivera's inquiry into whether or not Adele knew Lee Harvey Oswald. And Rivera's suggestion that Adele visit the Carousel Club in Dallas, owned by Jack Ruby.

Edisen denied knowing Oswald. Rivera told her that Oswald used to live in Russia, and now was in Dallas with his wife and child and is planning to visit New Orleans. Adele was from New Orleans, so Rivera encouraged Adele to get to know the Oswalds, saying they were a very lovely couple.

The following night, Rivera gave Edisen a tour of the city. As they approached the White House, Rivera commented, "I wonder what Jackie will do when her husband dies." Later that night, Rivera asked Adele to call Oswald when she returned to New Orleans and provided her with Oswald's telephone number, tel: 899-4244. Rivera asked

Edisen to give Oswald a message: *Kill the Chief.* Then claimed we were just playing a little joke on Oswald. Edisen was under the assumption that Oswald was a fellow scientist and friend of Dr. Rivera.

Edisen arrived in New Orleans and called Oswald as instructed. She spoke to Marina, Oswald's wife. She called back, and this time, Oswald answered the phone and said he didn't know who Jose Rivera was. So, she chose not to deliver the "Kill the Chief" instructions. Could Rivera be involved in a plot against President Kennedy? Fraught. Edison decided to contact the Secret Service in New Orleans and spoke to Special Agent J. Calvin Rice. Concerned the Secret Service might not believe her she cancelled the meeting. Edison later recounted this to FBI Special Agent Oren Bartlett.

Number 15

Thomas Mosely

U.S. Secret Service Memorandum Report #7-1-50, Synopsis: "Informant 2-1-266 has advised that one Thomas Mosely has been in touch with a group of Chicago Cubans who may be involved in the assassination of the late President John F. Kennedy."

On 21-Nov-1963, a Cuban exile named Homer Echevarria was negotiating the sale of guns with an Alcohol, Tobacco, and Firearms informant named Thomas Mosely. During this brokerage, Echevarria told the informant that they could close the arms deal "as we now have plenty of money–our new backers are Jews–as soon as we take care of Kennedy."

Number 16

Anonymous

In an anonymous phone call to Josh King and Ted Meadows at the KLAC news bureau in Los Angeles on 24-Nov-1963, an unidentified woman who worked at the Beverly Hilton Hotel in Beverly Hills–where JFK had stayed on his last trip to Los Angeles– said she was in a hotel elevator on 21-Nov-1963 at around 6:55 pm going to her workstation on the top floor. A man got on the elevator with her. She asked him what floor he was going to, and he replied that he was going with her to the top floor.

The man was reading a newspaper, and she asked him what the headlines were. The man replied, "Kennedy has been assassinated. Kennedy is dead." The woman said she didn't know what to make of the statement and so went about her work and then went home.

The next morning, 22-Nov-1963, the woman was awakened at home by a friend and told that President Kennedy had been assassinated. The woman believes she can identify the man, as only three persons checked out of the hotel on 22-Nov, including the man in the elevator. The man on the elevator has yet to be identified.

Number 17

John Martino

John Martino, an electronics expert, particularly specializing in the gambling machines employed in Havana casinos run by organized crime. Martino was arrested in Havana in July 1959 and spent three years in prison there. On his return to Florida, he became associated with Frank Sturgis, Eddie Bayo, and other anti-Castro activists. Martino also mentioned the not-well-known CIA officer Dave Morales in his book, *I Was Castro's Prisoner.*

In the spring and summer of 1963, Martino was heavily involved in the Bayo-Pawley raid (aka Operation TILT), an operation intended to smuggle out of Cuba two Russian officers who, it was said, wanted to defect and alert the world to the presence of Soviet missiles remaining in Cuba after the Missile Crisis. A team was landed but never returned.

Martino and an associate named Nathaniel Weyl were active in the aftermath of JFK's assassination, spreading a variety of stories intended to tie Lee Harvey Oswald to Fidel Castro.

Martino's confession was not confined to his wife and son, Eddie. In 1975, he told Newsday reporter John Cummings about his involvement in the JFK murder, serving as a courier, delivering money, etc.

He told a similar story to his business partner Fred Claasen that same year, as recounted in Tony Summer's book *Conspiracy*:

The anti-Castro people put Oswald together. Oswald didn't know who he was working for--he was just ignorant of who was really putting him together. Oswald was to meet his contact at the Texas Theatre. They were to meet Oswald in the theatre and get him out of the country, then eliminate him. Oswald made a mistake...There was no way we could get to him. They had Ruby kill him.

Number 18

Ralph Leon Yates

Did Ralph Leon Yates see Oswald bring the rifle to the Texas School Book Depository -- TSBD?

Cited from Article by **Jim Morrison**: Most Viewed Writer on WW2 and JFK Assassination.

The End of Innocence

Ralph Yates was a refrigeration mechanic for the Texas Butcher Supply Company in Dallas. On Nov. 20, 1963, two days before JFK's motorcade through the city, Yates picked up a hitchhiker in Oak Cliff near the Beckley Avenue entrance to the R L Thornton Expressway that went to Dallas. Beckley Avenue was the street that Oswald lived on, and after seeing Oswald in the news days after the assassination, Yates would tell the FBI that he gave Oswald a lift to the corner of Houston and Elm, which is the corner location of the TSBD. Not only that, this Oswald was carrying a brown paper-wrapped package that was four to four and a half feet long that the hitchhiker stated contained curtain rods. When Yates told the hitchhiker he could place the package in the back of the truck, the man insisted on keeping the package with him in the cab.

Now Yates, upon returning to the company's site told a co-worker about his hitchhiker, and later his wife also. But that is just the beginning of the story, as there is so much more. Yates was a talker and mentioned that President Kennedy would be in Dallas on Friday. The hitchhiker seemed eager to talk on this subject and then asked

133

Yates if he thought a person could assassinate the President. Yates was totally surprised by this question but said it was a possibility. Then, the rider got more specific, about whether it could be done from the top of a building or a high window. Yates replied that the shooter would need a scope and would have to be a good shot.

The rider then pulled out a picture of a man with a rifle and asked whether it could be done with a gun like this. As Yates was driving he didn't get a good look at the photo but ventured a guess that it was a possibility. The man asked Yates if he knew the President's motorcade route. Yates replied he didn't, but it was published in the newspapers. The rider then told Yates that he had misunderstood his question, asking whether the route could be changed. Yates said that it was highly unlikely to change the route except for safety reasons.

At this point, the rider asked to be let off at Houston and Elm, kitty-corner to the TSBD. He exited the cab with his long set of paper-wrapped curtain rods. After Yates had finished his callouts and returned to his workplace, he related his strange conversation to his co-worker, Demsey Jones. Jones thereby became a supporting witness that Yates had relayed his strange conversation ahead of the assassination about picking up a hitchhiker, especially the part where a person could be in a high building and shoot the President as he passed by.

On Nov. 26, Yates took the initiative and contacted the FBI, who weren't overly excited about Yates's story of giving Oswald, or an identical likeness, a ride to the TSBD with "curtain rods," which now suggested a rifle. Yates would be called back by the FBI 3 more times and finally was given a polygraph test in early January. Yates passed the test to the dismay of the FBI who wanted to discredit Yates, not wanting this to jeopardize the government case. Even if this lookalike was an Oswald double, it was too close for comfort for the FBI as this hitchhiker had been picked up on the same Beckley Avenue that the real Oswald lived on and let off at the place where the real Oswald worked. Then there was the "curtain rod" brown paper-wrapped package, which was the same as the cover story the FBI was using on how Oswald smuggled the Carcano rifle into the TSBD. The one thing that the FBI had in its favor was that Oswald had been working at the TSBD on the morning of the hitchhiker story.

Yates was not involved at all. He was simply a repairman for a company that fixes restaurant equipment. Yates was a young fella, about 24, and he already had five kids. The Secret Service told Yate's wife that her husband believes everything he's saying and he's convinced himself that all this happened. You need to take him to the psychiatric facility in Dallas immediately. And so she takes him to the hospital and they admit him. They kept him drugged up completely until he finally realized that he could take the pills under his tongue and take them out when the nurse left. He finally escaped from the asylum. With his wife and five kids, they moved around a lot, and she got to thinking that his paranoia was driving him nuts. So she turned him in. He spent 11 years back in that psychiatric facility, and he died there.

TASH P. ANESTOS
First Lieutenant

NUMBER 19

Peter Tash Anestos

There are no articles to cite on number 19. I found this guy and hardly anybody ever heard of him. Peter tells a 10-minute story about being in Greece with his father and overhearing a conversation between CIA agents about killing the president. His story can be found at JFK Theories by Jim Manning on YouTube:

https://www.youtube.com/watch?v=UdiWN-BqWDg

Peter's father was in charge of US military intelligence in Greece. Peter went to a party with his girlfriend, who was a nanny for the Secret Service station chief at his house. That night, they were conniving(?) in the grass outside when two men walked out of the house: the station chief from Athens and one from Marcus Greece. They were talking about Mr. Big and that Big was going to assassinate the president. Three guys from Italy were sent to Athens on a ferry, headed to northern Greece to meet the station chief for the CIA there, who was one of their best shooters. He was to train them.

Eventually, Peter tells his friend about this and goes crazy. Then everything dies down, and he comes back to the States to go to school. And then assassination occurs. He says all that time, I thought it was the president of Greece they were killing. His father later said to him, so now you know which President it was. And Oswald never killed anybody. He was the biggest stool pigeon that ever lived. Peter continued, I know a lot more. But I just wanted to get this off my chest before I die. I'm pretty old now. He was around 75, then died in 2021. But I'm glad he put it on there.

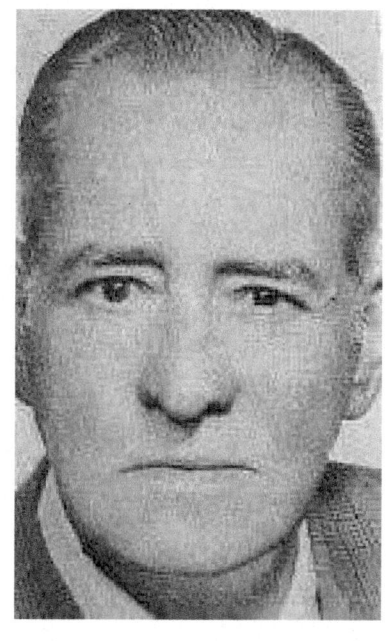

NUMBER 20

Willie Somersett

Right-wing extremist Joseph Milteer told Miami police informant William Somersett that the murder of JFK was "in the workings." At 94, former Miami Beach mayor and still active Miami-Dade Senior Judge Seymour Gelber is among the few who remember Miami police informant No. 88, Willie Augustus Somersett. "Willie was just a garrulous guy," said Gelber, who worked with Somersett while serving as a top assistant to Dade State Attorney Richard Gerstein in the 1960s...

You won't find Somersett's name in the 26 volumes published by the Warren Commission, the official government investigation that concluded Lee Harvey Oswald was Kennedy's lone assassin.

Yet 13 days before that dark day in Dallas, Somersett elicited a chilling, police tape-recorded threat from a right-wing racist who talked of how the President would soon be shot "from an office building with a high-powered rifle" and how "they'll pick up somebody within hours after...just to throw the public off."

Extremist Joseph A. Milteer of Quitman, Ga., made the threat against Kennedy in the kitchen of Somersett's small apartment in downtown Miami. Was it dumb luck or advanced knowledge? Milteer's uncanny prediction remains unexplained to this day.

In the late 1970s, the House Assassinations Committee had experts analyze a photograph taken in Dealey Plaza moments before the first shot of an unidentified motorcade spectator "who bears a strong resemblance" to Milteer. The experts, however, concluded the man was not Milteer, who died in 1974.

Events leading to Willie Somersett's Nov. 9, 1963, recorded talk with Milteer began 21 months earlier after a bomb exploded outside the home of *Miami Herald* Editor Don Shoemaker. The city's entire detective force was assigned to the case, according to news accounts at the time. Somersett, a part-time union organizer with right-wing ties and a track record as a paid FBI snitch, came forward to point the finger. Gelber credits the information he provided with leading authorities to identify and convict the bomber – a Nazi sympathizer who worked as a meter reader for the city of Miami.

Records show the FBI had dropped Somersett for a while as an informant in 1961 "for indiscretions...which threatened to expose a reliable Bureau informant." By 1963, however, the FBI had given him the code name "T-2," and reports described him as "a source who has furnished reliable information in the past."

It was at an April 1963 meeting in New Orleans of the Congress of Freedom Party, a confederation of right-wing political groups, where Somersett hooked up with Milteer, an old friend and a representative of the notoriously violent Dixie Klan faction of the Ku Klux Klan. Somersett saw Milteer again in Indianapolis in October at the convention of the far-right Constitution Party. As a member of that group's board of directors, Milteer helped formulate "plans to put an end to the Kennedy, (Martin Luther) King, Khrushchev dictatorship over our nation."

Gelber, the father of former State Sen. Dan Gelber, kept a diary back then about his work as a prosecutor. He wrote, "Somersett frequently uses the expression 'the most violent man I know'" to describe Milteer. "I am beginning to suspect he is intuitively separating the talkers from the doers."

Following the meeting in Indianapolis, Gelber suggested police tape-record Milteer during an upcoming trip to Miami. Detective Everett Kay, Somersett's police contact, set up a tape recorder in a broom closet in Somersett's residence in a building in the 1300 block of North Miami Avenue. Today, the former apartment building is a giant billboard.

"The FBI was tipped off about John F. Kennedy's assassination 13 days before the shooting but ignored it, according to a retired agent. Don Adams, 82, was involved in the official JFK murder investigation. He claims the Secret Service and FBI failed to properly investigate a right-wing extremist who was recorded saying how the President would soon be shot 'from an office building with a high-powered rifle' and how 'they'll pick up somebody within hours after…just to throw the public off.'

In his 2012 book, 'From an Office Building with a High-Powered Rifle,' Adams claims the FBI had enough information to stop President Kennedy and his wife from traveling. He also claims he was only allowed to ask Milteer five generic questions after the shooting, thwarting a proper investigation, the Miami Herald reports. Milteer was not interrogated about his previously recorded statements to Somersett regarding plans to murder the president nor asked where he was on the day of the murder.

The Secret Service and the FBI kept the recordings a secret from the public for three years after the assassination. In 1978, the U.S. House of Representatives Assassinations Committee conducted a limited investigation of Milteer and published a portion of the transcript of Milteer's recorded conversation with Somersett. The committee found Milteer's threat 'was ignored by Secret Service personnel in planning the trip to Dallas. Word of Milteer's threat may even have reached President Kennedy himself.

Somersett told the Miami Police that Milteer was jubilant about Kennedy's death. He said, 'Well, I told you so. It happened like I told you, didn't it?'" Somersett said, according to one report. I said, 'That's right. I don't know whether you were guessing or not, but you hit it on the head pretty good.' He said, 'Well, that is the way it was supposed to be done, and that is the way it was done."

Chapter 11

The Catch & Kill Mighty Wurlitzer

Frank Gardner Wisner, head of the CIA's Clandestine Operations Directorate, liked to boast of his powerful connections with the American media, claiming that he could plant any story he wanted in the major American newspapers. He also claimed he could prevent the publication of any article or book that he felt reflected negatively on the CIA.

Wisner called this his "Mighty Wurlitzer." Wisner and his associates could powerfully influence American perceptions and completely silence any media opposition with a judicious mixture of bribery, special favors, and outright cash payments. Prominent academics, revered newspaper columnists, historical writers, newspaper and magazine editors, book publishers, and, later, television executives all gorged at the CIA trough.

When one died, there were many eager to take his place. In the 1996 list received from Robert Crowley, one of Wisner's senior executives, among others, are politely termed CIA "sources." These published names include Tim Golden and Ivar Peterson of the New York Times, Howard Kurz and Walter Pincus of the Washington Post, Doyle McManus of the Los Angeles Times, Ted Koppel of the Nightline television program, Professor Timothy Naftali of Yale University and significant number of other members of the media, the business world, and academia.

It is an illustrative example of the methods the CIA uses to either plant stories favorable to the agency or to kill the reputations of those who produce unfavorable material. The agency has a standing policy of completely ignoring any criticism of its actions or purported actions. They attack their enemies through their many surrogates and avid supporters in the American and foreign media. The CIA rarely engages in disputes with someone who questions its actions. They activate the Wisner media Wurlitzer to considerable effect. Ultimately, the "Company" (as its initiates call it) claims plausible denial if some irrefutable proof surfaces.

The CIA personnel, whose task is to review published material that might interest them, will read it if a friendly media member can get the publisher to give them a free "review" copy. There will be no immediate response on their part because the work has to filter, at the very least, through a study group or, if it is considered a serious public relations menace, a committee.

Several months will elapse, and the study group or committee will report to senior levels of internal influence. During this period of investigative gestation, no public comments will be forthcoming other than frantic requests to friends in the media to ignore the work and make no comment of any kind on either the work or its author.

Suppose the work contains serious allegations backed with documentary evidence. In that case, the CIA will determine the potential damage if the work gains significant circulation. CIA damage control will beckon an eager media friend to prepare another book that would completely demolish the thesis of the first unacceptable work. Once this literary antidote was in progress, supportive documents would be located in official archives and deliberately misinterpreted or forged, and a CIA media campaign of ridicule would be launched against the offending author, not his work. The work must never be reviewed lest someone might read it. The CIA will invent creative works of fiction like the author endangered motorists by crossing a street against a light. Overdue library books would translate into "attempted theft" and "conversion of government property." Retail book outlets are asked not to stock a book that would never receive a positive media review.

The book Regicide, released in 2001, which included Robert Crowley's documents, suffered this CIA fate. The publisher is no longer in business. I am confident the CIA of 2024 is not the Wurlitzer CIA of 1963. Some of Crowley's memos and documents are reprinted here to give us all the answers to who killed JFK.

Chapter 12

Manning's Conclusions

This work culminates over 55 years of my research, investigation, and analysis of the John F. Kennedy assassination. I believe it will stand the test of time. The government agencies have done their best to hide any evidence contrary to the Alice in Wonderland adventure they contrived some 60 years ago. The JFK execution was limited to a small rogue group in what was otherwise a patriotic, well-intentioned organization of thousands of hard-working individuals who were unaware of the treachery of a few at the top. That goes for the FBI as well as the Joint Chiefs of Staff.

The concept I find puzzling is that at this moment in history, all of the conspirators are dead and gone now, and it's time to settle the killer question responsibly. I am calling for a public referendum on a new and final congressional investigation to air the dirty acts of men long gone to exonerate Oswald.

Any serious individuals who have spent time on this conundrum for decades agree on two facts. One: Lee Harvey Oswald was, as he said, a patsy. Two: Oswald was the scapegoat patsy of the CIA, FBI, DCI, and JCS to serve their quorum decision to sentence John F. Kennedy and his brother to death for treason with no congressional oversight. All records of Oswald's interrogation, carried out by the Dallas police and the Secret Service, were subsequently destroyed without a trace. Anything or anyone that conflicted with the Warren Commission Report work of fiction no longer exists except for the documents saved by the assassination plotters, which I felt beholden to reproduce in this book.

NARA worked with the agencies to jointly review the remaining redactions in 3,648 JFK documents in compliance with President Biden's directive. In June 2023, NARA posted 2,672 documents containing newly released information.

History will prove that American transparency and the rule of law work in a democracy. No one is above the law, not the President nor those who work for him, whom we pay with our tax dollars.

Amid the hundreds of books and millions of words written on JFK, I have heard the phrase, "But somebody would have talked." Well, somebody did, but nobody is listening. Robert Turnbull Crowley, The Crow, saw himself and the other wolves involved in the plot as Patriots. The Crow didn't confess; he was proud of his work. He was sad when his friends at Langley did not keep in touch after his retirement.

I ask you to consider these five thoughts:

1. If you know that more than 20+ people knew of the assassination in advance and tried to stop it, it must be a conspiracy.

2. If you know that more than 20 professional hitmen were either filmed or arrested in   Dealy   Plaza   on November 22nd, 1963, it must be a conspiracy.

3. If over 50 witnesses died in very suspicious ways before they could testify their knowledge of the assassination in court, it must be a conspiracy.

4. If a top-ranking CIA official would turn over his notes, files, letters, and top-secret material to a writer to tell the truth after his death, it must be a conspiracy.

5. If the intelligence agencies buy up all the printed books to prevent reprints of the last piece of the conundrum from being published, it must be a conspiracy.

What do you believe?

Together, can we prevent this history from repeating itself?

AUTHOR

JAMES MANNING

Jim Manning served in the Marines when John F. Kennedy was assassinated. After he called New Orleans district attorney Jim Garrison in 1968 to share an important fact regarding the conspiracy to assassinate JFK, Manning's life was threatened. For fifty-five years since, Manning has researched every angle of Lee Harvey Oswald's involvement and who killed Kennedy, applying his knowledge of the law from the Virginia Bar Association Reading Program, successful tenure selling law books to attorneys at Matthew Bender and Co., and as a licensed private investigator. This book is a culmination of Manning's lifelong pursuit of justice. As a Marine, Semper Fidelis, always faithful, it is Manning's honor to exonerate Lee Harvey Oswald of the JFK murder.

Manning is a beloved community member; he is civil-minded and goes out of his way to help others. He lives with his wonderful wife in Norfolk, Virginia. He is a proud father and grandfather, a successful small business owner many times over, and serves as an advisor to other small business owners.